SAGE has been part of the global academic community since 1965, supporting high quality research and learning that transforms society and our understanding of individuals, groups and cultures. SAGE is the independent, innovative, natural home for authors, editors and societies who share our commitment and passion for the social sciences.

Find out more at: **www.sagepublications.com**

CONSTRUCTING RESEARCH QUESTIONS

DOING INTERESTING RESEARCH

MATS ALVESSON & JÖRGEN SANDBERG

Los Angeles | London | New Delhi
Singapore | Washington DC

Los Angeles | London | New Delhi
Singapore | Washington DC

SAGE Publications Ltd
1 Oliver's Yard
55 City Road
London EC1Y 1SP

SAGE Publications Inc.
2455 Teller Road
Thousand Oaks, California 91320

SAGE Publications India Pvt Ltd
B 1/I 1 Mohan Cooperative Industrial Area
Mathura Road
New Delhi 110 044

SAGE Publications Asia-Pacific Pte Ltd
3 Church Street
#10-04 Samsung Hub
Singapore 049483

Editor: Kirsty Smy
Editorial assistant: Nina Smith
Production editor: Sarah Cooke
Marketing manager: Alison Borg
Cover design: Lisa Harper
Typeset by: C&M Digitals (P) Ltd, Chennai, India
Printed and bound by CPI Group (UK) Ltd,
Croydon, CR0 4YY

© Mats Alvesson and Jörgen Sandberg 2013

First published 2013

Apart from any fair dealing for the purposes of research or private study, or criticism or review, as permitted under the Copyright, Designs and Patents Act, 1988, this publication may be reproduced, stored or transmitted in any form, or by any means, only with the prior permission in writing of the publishers, or in the case of reprographic reproduction, in accordance with the terms of licences issued by the Copyright Licensing Agency. Enquiries concerning reproduction outside those terms should be sent to the publishers.

Library of Congress Control Number: 2012944430

British Library Cataloguing in Publication data

A catalogue record for this book is available from the British Library

ISBN 978-1-44625-592-6
ISBN 978-1-44625-593-3 (pbk)

Contents

About the authors — vi

Preface — vii

1 Research questions: a core ingredient in developing interesting theories — 1

2 The context of constructing and formulating research questions — 10

3 Gap-spotting: the prevalent way of constructing research questions in social science — 24

4 A critical evaluation of gap-spotting research: does it lead to interesting theories? — 38

5 Problematization as a methodology for generating research questions — 47

6 Applying the problematization methodology in practice — 71

7 Why does gap-spotting dominate when it reduces the chance to create interesting theories? — 92

8 Constructing interesting research questions: problematization and beyond — 111

Appendices — 124

References — 129

Index — 139

About the Authors

Mats Alvesson is Professor of Business Administration at the University of Lund, Sweden, and a part-time professor in the school of Business at the University of Queensland, Australia. He has published a large number of books on a variety of topics, including *Reflexive Methodology* (with Kaj Sköldberg, Sage, 2009, Second edition), *Understanding Organizational Culture* (Sage, 2012, Second edition), *Understanding Gender and Organization* (with Yvonne Billing, Sage, 2009, Second edition), *Knowledge Work and Knowledge-Intensive Firms* (Oxford University Press, 2004) and *Changing Organizational Culture* (with Stefan Sveningsson, Routledge, 2008), as well as *Interpreting Interviews* (Sage, 2011), *Qualitative Research and Theory Development* (with Dan Kärreman, Sage, 2011) and *Metaphors We Lead By* (edited with André Spicer, Routledge, 2011).

Jörgen Sandberg is Professor in the School of Business at the University of Queensland, Australia. His research interests include competence and learning in organizations, leadership, practice-based theories, qualitative research methods and the philosophical underpinnings of organizational research. He is currently carrying out research on practice theory in organization studies, frameworks and methodologies for developing more interesting and relevant theories and sense making in organizations. His work has appeared in numerous journals including the *Academy of Management Journal*, *Academy of Management Review*, *Harvard Business Review*, *Journal of Management Studies*, *Organisational Research Methods* and *Organization Studies*. He is also the author of several books and book chapters on the above topics published by Sage, Thomson, Routledge, and Kluwer.

Preface

As we demonstrate in this book, there is a widely felt shortage of interesting and novel ideas in social science. Much contemporary research is perceived to lack imagination and to offer little new theoretical insight. This is perhaps partly related to the fact that much has already been said in most disciplines, which makes it difficult to come up with anything radically new. Nevertheless, the lack of research contributions that stand out as interesting and exert a broader influence can also be viewed as an outcome of strong and narrow specialization coupled with a tendency for researchers to reproduce taken-for-granted assumptions and established vocabularies in their respective fields. The need to publish in the right journals and careers informed by 'publish or perish' orientations associated with the contemporary age of not only mass education but also mass research make many people unwilling to work with deviant ideas. As we will try to demonstrate, there are strong forces towards mainstreaming in many, if not most, academic fields. Established methodologies and norms for producing and publishing research tend to emphasize and normalize narrow and cautious research questions.

In this book we address this issue and try to make a case for an alternative way of approaching the subject matter under study. We highlight and focus on the theme of research questions. This is a neglected theme in much of the writing concerning how to produce good research. Key elements in the construction of research questions – which we see as a crucial element in, and a significant driver of, research and results – are the critical investigation and challenging of established assumptions in an area. Establishing and working with new assumptions opens up possibilities for producing more interesting and influential research, especially the development of new theoretical ideas. This book offers a rationale, a methodology and illustrations for such work. In addition, we also address how institutions, professional norms and researchers' identity obstruct or facilitate more imaginative, challenging and interesting work. The quality and character of research is very much a matter of social norms; institutional forces framing the ways researchers do research.

This book is partly based on a series of articles we have published already. Chapters 3 and 4 are partly revisions and an extension of Sandberg, J. and Alvesson, M. (2011) 'Routes to research questions: beyond gap-spotting', *Organization*, 18: 22–44. Chapters 5 and the first half of Chapter 6 build on Alvesson, M. and Sandberg, J. (2011) 'Generating research questions through problematization', *Academy of Management Review*, 36: 247–71, and Chapter 7 is a revision of Alvesson, M. and Sandberg, J. (2012) 'Has management studies lost its way? Ideas for more imaginative and innovative research', *Journal of Management Studies*. We are grateful to the publishers of these journals for allowing us to use the material in this book, and to the editors and the reviewers of these journal articles for their good advice.

We also are highly appreciative of the comments on drafts of this book from three anonymous reviewers consulted by SAGE Publications and from our colleagues Ronald Barnett, Alan Burton-Jones, Peter Liesch, Allan Luke, Tyler Okimoto and Sverre Spoelstra. This book has also benefitted from research collaborations over the years with, in the case of MA, Stan Deetz, Dan Kärreman and Kaj Sköldberg, and for JS, Gloria Dall'Alba and Hari Tsoukas.

Lund and Brisbane, June 2012
Mats Alvesson and Jörgen Sandberg

1

RESEARCH QUESTIONS: A CORE INGREDIENT IN DEVELOPING INTERESTING THEORIES

Research in the social sciences takes many different forms and is guided by several different objectives. Some researchers aim for prediction and explanation while others search for understanding. Sometimes empirical description and accuracy are central; sometimes these are subordinated to theoretical ambitions. In certain cases researchers try to develop theory through careful empirical investigations; in others the fieldwork is exploratory and aims to trigger theoretical inspiration; and in some instances empirical investigation is bypassed all together by pure armchair theorization. Despite the huge variety in research styles within the social sciences, there is broad consensus about the importance of generating original and significant theoretical contributions. A theoretical contribution offers insights that clearly go beyond the diligent reporting of empirical findings and the validation of established knowledge. In particular, as researchers, most of us want to produce not only credible empirical results and revisions of theories but also interesting and influential ideas and theories.

A fundamental step in all theory development is the formulation of carefully grounded research questions. Constructing and formulating research questions is one of the most, perhaps the most, critical aspects of all research. Without posing questions it is not possible to develop our knowledge about a particular subject. One could even say that good research questions might be as valuable and sometimes even more valuable than answers. Questions may open up, encourage reflection and trigger intellectual activity; answers may lead to the opposite: to rest and closure. Good research questions, however, do not just exist they also need to be created and formulated. As many scholars have pointed out it is particularly important to produce innovative questions which 'will open up new research problems, might resolve long-standing controversies, could provide an integration of different approaches, and might even turn conventional wisdom and assumptions upside down by challenging old beliefs' (Campbell et al., 1982: 21; and see Abbott, 2004; Astley, 1985; Bruner, 1996; Davis, 1971, 1986). In other words, if we do not pose innovative research questions, it is less likely that our research efforts will generate interesting and influential theories. A novel research question may be what distinguishes exceptional from mediocre research and the production of trivial results. Yet, despite the importance of posing innovative questions, little attention has been paid to how this can be accomplished.

In this book we argue that problematization – in the sense of questioning the assumptions underlying existing theory in some significant ways – is fundamental to the construction of innovative research questions and, thus, to the development of interesting and influential theories. We define both research questions and theory quite broadly. Research questions concern the input and direction of a study, defining what a study is about and reflecting the curiosity of the researcher. Theory is about concepts and relationships between concepts offering a deeper understanding of a range of empirical instances. Theory for us overlaps with ideas – in this book we focus more on the overall theoretical idea than on the fine-tuning of a theoretical framework.

Several factors will influence the development of research questions (such as research funding, publication opportunities, fashion and fieldwork experience), which we will discuss further in Chapter 2. In this book we concentrate on one core aspect, namely, how researchers can construct research questions from *existing academic literature* that will lead to the development of interesting and influential theories. Existing literature can be seen to summarize and express the knowledge and the thinking of the academic community – and to some extent of our time, as there is an overlap in many areas between academic knowledge and broader knowledge shared by educated people more generally. Existing academic literature refers both to the theoretical perspectives and the substantive (empirical) studies conducted within the subject area targeted. A theoretical perspective and an empirical domain may overlap (that is, when a theory is closely linked to a domain, such as classroom theory). However, in other instances they may be more loosely linked, such as when 'grand theories' or master perspectives (for example, Marxism, symbolic interactionism, Foucauldian power/knowledge) are applicable to a wide range of subject matters.

Although not many studies have specifically looked at how researchers construct research questions from existing theory and studies, several have come close. For example, Davis's (1971, 1986) research about what defines interesting and famous theories; Campbell et al.'s (1982) investigation of the antecedents of significant (and less significant) research findings; Abbott's (2004) suggestion of using heuristics for generating new research ideas; Starbuck's (2006) advice that researchers should challenge their own thinking through various disruption tactics, including ambitions to take other views than the one favored one into account; and Yanchar et al.'s (2008) study of the components of critical thinking practice in research.

Although these studies point to important ingredients in constructing research questions, they do not specifically focus on how researchers arrive at, or at least claim to have arrived at, their research questions. For example, although Becker (1998) and Abbott (2004) provide a whole range of tricks and heuristics for generating research ideas, those tricks and heuristics 'are not specifically aimed at any particular phase or aspect of the research process' (Abbott, 2004: 112). Existing studies focus even less on the ways of constructing research questions from existing literature that are likely to facilitate the development of interesting and influential theories.

Similarly, in most standard textbooks on research methods the actual ways of constructing research questions are scantly treated or not discussed at all (Flick, 2006). Instead, the primary discussion revolves around how to formulate feasible research questions in a particular sequential order. We are advised to first define the topic (for example, leadership, adult vocational learning, diversity among male engineers, middle-class status anxiety in UK higher education institutions, attitudes to group sex among mature students), then to clarify the domain of the research, that is, what objects should be studied (individuals, social interaction, and so on), state a purpose and finally to decide the type of research questions, such as descriptive, explanatory and prescriptive questions. Some textbooks (for example, Silverman, 2001; Van de Ven, 2007) advise that formulating good research questions does not only involve defining domain, topic, purpose and type of question. It also involves considering contextual issues, such as how various stakeholders, the background and experience of the researcher and the field of study, may influence the formulation of research questions. While important, such advice does not provide specific directions on ways to formulate innovative research questions by scrutinizing existing literature in a particular research area. We will therefore only briefly address such advice. Instead, we will concentrate on what we see as the key issues around constructing research questions from the existing literature that are likely to lead to more interesting and influential theories within the social sciences. In particular, we argue that in order to construct novel research questions from existing literature, careful attention, critical scrutiny, curiosity and imagination together with the cultivation of a more reflexive and inventive scholarship are needed. We hope that this book will contribute to achieving such an endeavor.

A paradoxical shortage of high-impact research

The need to better understand how to construct innovative research questions from the existing literature appears to be particularly pertinent today, as there is growing concern about an increasing shortage of more interesting and influential studies in many disciplines within the social sciences (Abbott, 2004; Becker, 1998; Gibbons et al., 1994; Richardson and Slife, 2011; Slife and Williams, 1995). For example, many prominent sociologists, such as Ritzer (1998) and Stacey (1999), are concerned that sociology has 'gone astray' (Weinstein, 2000: 344) in the sense that most sociological research is increasingly specialized, narrow and incremental, and therefore not 'likely to interest a larger audience' (Ritzer, 1998: 447). Similarly, in our own field, the outgoing editors of the *Journal of Management Studies* noted in their concluding editorial piece – based on their review of more than 3000 manuscripts during their six years in office (2003–2008) – that while submissions had increased heavily '… it is hard to conclude that this has been accompanied by a corresponding increase in papers that add significantly to the discipline. More is being produced but the big impact papers remain elusive …' (Clark and Wright, 2009: 6).

The perceived shortage of influential ideas and theories, that is, those reaching beyond a narrow and specialized area, is paradoxical in the sense that more research than ever is being conducted and published within the social sciences. The increased use of research assessment reviews in many countries (for example, RAE/REF in the UK and ERA in Australia) and of designated journal lists for evaluating research performance is a central driver behind the rapid growth of articles published within the social sciences. Not only has the number of published journal articles increased substantially but also the competition to get published. Most journals' acceptance rates have been steadily shrinking and are now close to 5% in many top-tier journals. Publishing in these journals is typically a very long and tedious process, involving numerous revisions before getting the final decision, which is usually a rejection. Given all this, one would expect a relative increase in high-quality research, leading to more interesting and influential theories being published. Paradoxically, this is not the case. Quality may have risen in some respects, but hardly the number of interesting and influential theories. Rather than innovation and creativity, it is technical competence and the discipline to carry out incremental research that seem to dominate all the hard-working researchers within the social sciences.

What differentiates an interesting from a non-interesting theory?

But why does incremental research rarely seem to generate high-impact theories? In order to answer this question we need first to understand what makes a theory interesting. That is, how a theory attracts attention from other researchers and the educated public, leads to enthusiasm, 'aha' and 'wow' moments, and triggers responses like 'I have not thought about this before' or 'Perhaps I should rethink this theme'.

While different people may find different theories interesting and it is a fact that very few theories are seen as interesting by everybody, interestingness is hardly just a matter of idiosyncratic opinion (Das and Long, 2010). Collectively held assessments of what counts as interesting research are much more prevalent than purely subjective views, even though the collective can be restricted to a sub-community (interested in say sexual harassment at a nightclub or Muslim immigrants in Belfast) rather than an entire field (such as higher education or leisure studies).

During the last four decades, originating with Davis's (1971) seminal sociological study, a large number of researchers have shown that rigorously executed research is typically not enough for a theory to be regarded as interesting and influential: it must also challenge an audience's taken-for-granted assumptions in some significant way (Astley, 1985; Bartunek et al., 2006; Hargens, 2000; Weick, 2001). In other words, if a theory does not challenge some of an audience's assumptions, it is unlikely to receive attention and become influential, even if it has been rigorously developed and has received a lot of empirical support. This insight has meant that the criterion of 'interestingness' in most top-tier journals has 'become a staple for editorial descriptions of desired papers' (Corley and Gioia, 2011: 11). We are, however, as we will come back to, skeptical as to the scope and depth of the actual use of this criterion in many situations, as other more conservative criteria often seem to carry more weight for some, if not most, journals (we offer support for this claim in Chapter 7).

Arguably, there are also other reasons or mechanisms than interestingness for why a theory becomes influential in the sense of garnering citations and sometimes even becoming well known in the public domain. For example, a theory's influence can be related to power relations within academia where a dominant coalition can more or less dictate mainstream, imitation tendencies and fashion following. A theory can also be ideologically appealing and serve broader political interests that are willing to generously fund the 'right' kind of research. The impact and success of a theory may also be dependent on how easy it is to grasp and apply the credentials of its proposer(s) and to what extent it is in line with existing political and social values (Peter and Olson, 1986).

Hence, the answer to why a theory becomes influential is not always because it is seen as interesting but also related to other factors. We shall not venture into this complex area, merely emphasize that a theory regarded by fellow academics and intellectual members of the public as interesting is more likely to become influential in academic disciplines and sometimes also more broadly in society. The fact that other factors than 'interestingness' determine influence does of course not diminish the significance of 'interestingness' as a key element in a theory being influential. Our focus in the book is on the combination of interesting and influential. Therefore, theories that some people find interesting but which do not attract a larger audience and theories that are influential but which are not considered to be particularly interesting both fall outside our primary focus.

From gap-spotting to problematization

If interesting theories are those that challenge the assumptions of existing literature, *problematization* of the assumptions underlying existing theories appears to be a central ingredient in constructing and formulating research questions. However, established ways of generating research questions rarely express more ambitious and systematic attempts to challenge the assumptions underlying existing theories (Abbott, 2004; Locke and Golden-Biddle, 1997; Slife and Williams, 1995). Instead, they mainly try to identify or create gaps in the existing literature that need to be filled. It is common to refer either positively or mildly critically to earlier studies in order to 'fill this gap' (Lüscher and Lewis, 2008: 221) or 'to address this major gap in the literature' (Avery and Rendall, 2002: 3). Similarly, researchers often motivate their projects with formulations such as 'no other studies have examined the associations between children's belief and task-avoidant behaviour … which is the focus of the present study' (Mägi et al., 2011: 665) or 'our goal in this study was to address these important gaps by focusing on the effects of the group-level beliefs about voice' (Morrison et al., 2011). Such 'gap-spotting' seems to dominate most of the disciplines in social science, or at least management, sociology, psychology and education – areas that we have chosen as samples for illuminating broader conventions in social science. Gap-spotting means that the assumptions underlying existing literature for the most part remain unchallenged in the formulation of research questions. In other words, gap-spotting tends to *under-problematize* the existing literature and, thus, reinforces rather than challenges already influential theories.

There are, however, an increasing number of research orientations that directly or indirectly encourage problematization, such as certain versions of social constructionism, postmodernism, feminism and critical theory. Since the primary aim for many of these orientations is to disrupt rather than build upon and extend an established body of literature, it could be argued that they tend to *over-problematize* the research undertaken. In particular, these orientations tend to emphasize the 'capacity to disturb and threaten the stability of positive forms of management science' (Knights, 1992: 533) as a way to highlight what is 'wrong' (for example, misleading or dangerous) with existing knowledge (Deetz, 1996), that is, 'negative' knowledge is the aim (deconstruction being the ideal). This is often interesting and valuable but such 'tearing down' may also be tiresome after some time. For a large majority of researchers with a more 'positive' research agenda that aims to advance knowledge of a specific subject matter, such over-problematization is often seen as inappropriate and unhelpful (Rorty, 1992). In addition, a lot of disturbance-specialized research, which could be referred to as programmatic problematization, tends (after some time) to reproduce its own favored assumptions and thereby lose its capacity to provide novel problematizations. Nevertheless, we do consider this kind of research to offer valuable resources to challenge the assumptions of various literatures.

Aim of the book

The primary aim of this book is to integrate the positive and the negative research agenda by developing and proposing problematization as a *methodology* for identifying and challenging assumptions that underlie existing theories and, based on that, generating research questions that will lead to the development of more interesting and influential theories within social science. Such a problematization methodology enables researchers to embark on a more interesting and rewarding course (although perhaps also more difficult and risky) than following established and conventional routes for producing knowledge in a safe and predictable way.

A key theme in the book is a general argumentation for, and the offering of, a *framework* and *vocabulary* with which to conduct more interesting and influential studies, to indicate pitfalls as well as possibilities. In particular, this book suggests a reframing of the research practice within the social sciences by proposing a revision of how we approach research questions: from gap-spotting to assumption-challenging, from reproducing to disrupting the use of taken-for-granted beliefs and points of departure in inquiries. This revision not only concerns changes in theory and methodology it also encompasses social and political aspects. Research never takes place in a social vacuum and revised views of what is good research call for consideration of the social context, as well as how researchers define themselves in the research process.

In order to explore our key themes we investigate and answer the following questions: (1) How do social researchers produce their research questions? (2) What norms guide the production of research questions? And (3) What is seen as leading to interesting and influential theories? Based on those investigations, we develop and propose problematization as a methodology to challenge assumptions and to develop research questions that are more likely to lead to interesting theories. Specifically, we develop (1) a typology of what *types* of assumptions can be problematized in existing theories and propose (2) a set of methodological principles for *how* this can be done. We also provide (3) detailed examples of problematization and the formulation of novel, often counter-intuitive, research questions that can encourage more imaginative empirical studies.

This problematization methodology is the book's core contribution, and also the main theme for Chapters 5 and 6. But in order to increase the chances of doing more imaginative, interesting and (theoretically) influential research, we also need to understand the mechanisms behind doing less interesting work (which are the focus in Chapters 3 and 4). Moreover, we develop a framework for understanding the forces within academia that work *against* the research ideal we (and to a degree all of us) embrace and illuminate the significance of researchers' *identities* and ethos in knowledge production. Here, we emphasize the need for researchers to think through the purpose of their research and knowledge contributions and to resist pressures to adapt to dominant assumptions and be normalized, as well as normalizing others (Foucault, 1980).

We focus on problematizing assumptions that underlie *existing literature* as a way to construct research questions. We define research questions quite broadly; they not only indicate the delivery of a specific intended result, they also provide the broader framing of the study, that is, its overall direction and line of reasoning based on a set of assumptions and 'truths' already inscribed on the discourse guiding the inquiry. In other words, research questions give the major input, frame the research and provide direction-setting to research studies and, thus, form a key element of the research process. Therefore, research questions and the way they are addressed need to incorporate reflexivity in the sense of an explicit questioning and articulation of where the chosen research approach originates, where it is heading and what may be problematic about it.

We only briefly discuss how other aspects of the research process, such as a general interest in policy, institutional stakeholders and public debate, relevance for practitioners, choice of empirical case and unexpected empirical findings, may influence the research objective and, thus, the formulation of research questions. There is also a large and overlapping literature on reflexivity dealing with these aspects of research (Alvesson and Sköldberg, 2009; Steier, 1991) that is highly significant (although its relative importance varies between research projects). However, as our emphasis is on how to work with reflexivity when formulating research questions, we only marginally address other issues of reflexivity, such as invoking self-awareness in the researcher, the role of rhetoric and ongoing constructions of reality in the research process. An exception is the socio-political context of research, which is a key issue for how researchers relate to existing work (Alvesson, Hardy and Harley, 2008). Therefore, problematization studies need to seriously consider how other researchers may be skeptical of or even hostile towards research challenging their (favored) assumptions. We specifically deal with this issue in Chapter 7.

How this book is organized

In this chapter we have tried to place the book in the broader context of research methodology and argue for much more care in the critical investigation of how research questions are formulated and how theoretical inspiration can be used in the formulation of research questions. In particular, we have issued a warning against the risk of uncritically reproducing a set of assumptions that underlie the existing literature and may no longer be very productive and interesting when constructing research questions. We contend that this is common practice and that there is a shortage of novel thinking in many fields within social science.

In Chapter 2 we further elaborate on our quest to examine how researchers can generate research questions from existing literature by situating the research more precisely in the larger context of constructing and formulating research questions. We start by defining in what sense questions are crucial in knowledge development. We then discuss more specifically what makes a question a research question, what major types of research questions exist, from where research questions originate, and what influences the framing of research questions. Finally, we summarize the chapter by discussing the main stages involved in constructing and formulating research questions.

Subsequently in Chapters 3 and 4, we present an empirical study of how researchers typically construct their research questions from existing literature by systematically reviewing 10 leading journals from four different disciplines within the social sciences (management, sociology, psychology, and education). We also refer to some studies in other fields and how we can make a case for a common state of play across the social sciences as a whole. Our findings suggest that the most widespread way of producing research questions is that which we label gap-spotting, namely, to spot various gaps in existing literature, such as an overlooked area and, based on those gaps, formulate specific research questions. We provide a typology of gap-spotting and critically discuss the limitations and problems of gap-spotting research. In particular, we argue that gap-spotting questions are unlikely to lead to significant contributions because they do not question the assumptions which underlie the existing literature in any substantive way.

Chapter 5 develops from this starting point. We elaborate and propose problematization as an alternative methodology for generating research questions in three steps. First, we describe the aim and focal point of the methodology, as challenging the assumptions underlying existing literature. Second, we elaborate a typology consisting of five broad types of assumptions that are open for problematization in existing theory. Finally, we develop a set of methodological principles for identifying, articulating and challenging the assumptions underlying existing literature.

In Chapter 6 we illustrate how the developed problematization methodology can be used to generate research questions by applying it to two key texts within the social sciences. One is Dutton, Dukerich and Harquail's well-known (1994) article about organizational identity and identification with workplaces. The second is West and Zimmerman's (1987) classic work 'Doing gender'.

In Chapter 7 we critically discuss why gap-spotting is common and assumption challenging is rare despite increasing recognition that the latter leads to the development of more interesting and influential theories. We point to three broad and interacting drivers: institutional conditions; professional norms; and researchers' identity construction. We also elucidate possible solutions at a variety of levels, arguing for changes in terms of institutional and organizational structures and practices, revisions of the norms of academic publishing and the need for academics to reconsider their identities and methodological ideals. In particular, in contrast to the prevalent opportunistic maximization of getting published in high-ranking journals and climbing the academic career ladder as fast as possible and support for this in managerialist universities, we draw attention to the centrality of developing a more reflexive and inventive scholarship for universities and researchers.

In Chapter 8 we summarize the general argument of the book. We begin by elaborating on the major contributions the problematization methodology can make to social science. Thereafter, we briefly discuss in which situations the problematization methodology may be particularly relevant. Finally, we relate the problematization methodology to the overall research process and discuss how the problematization of existing literature can be complemented by empirical material in constructing and formulating novel research questions.

2
THE CONTEXT OF CONSTRUCTING AND FORMULATING RESEARCH QUESTIONS

As we argued in Chapter 1, most standard textbooks on research methods in the social sciences do not discuss (Denzin and Lincoln, 2011; Freebody, 2003) or only barely discuss (Hesse-Biber and Leavy, 2011; Silverman, 2001) the actual ways of constructing and formulating research questions (a notable exception is White, 2009). Even less attention is given to how research questions are constructed from existing literature and practically nothing is written about how to construct innovative research questions that are likely to lead to the development of more interesting and influential theories.

In Chapters 3 and 4 we specifically investigate how researchers construct research questions from existing literature. This is followed up in Chapters 5 and 6 where we provide an extensive elaboration of how to facilitate sharper and more imaginative research questions. As a background to those investigations, our aim in this chapter is to situate our study more precisely in the larger context of constructing and formulating research questions. We begin by exploring the role that questions play in knowledge development. Thereafter we look more specifically at what makes a question a research question, the major types of research questions that can be asked, where research questions originate from and the major factors that influence the framing of research questions. Finally, we distinguish the main stages and steps involved in constructing and formulating research questions from existing literature.

The priority of the question in knowledge development

It may seem odd and perhaps even rude to ask about the role that questions play in developing knowledge, as most textbooks about research methodology rarely devote any space to it. Perhaps they regard it as too obvious or not important enough. Or they may think there are endless ways of coming up with research questions and therefore find it difficult to say something meaningful about it. With the risk of stating the obvious, therefore, we think it is critical to spell out an answer, one which is simple but fundamental: questions are the core ingredient in all knowledge development.

As Gadamer states, 'the path of all knowledge leads through the question' (1994: 363). Questions provide the necessary starting point and path for all forms of knowledge development. It is by asking questions that we are able to generate knowledge about things. Similarly, asking questions forms the basis of every kind of research investigation. In order to find out how students learn, educational researchers need to pose specific questions, such as whether class size matters in learning and how students will go about learning specific ideas and topics. Likewise, in order to find out how humans think, act and behave in particular ways psychology researchers need to ask specific questions about human cognition and emotion. Hence, without asking questions it is not possible to develop any knowledge, or at least not valuable knowledge. Research questions therefore provide the inevitable and necessary starting point for, and have the priority in, all forms of scientific knowledge development. They provide the basic direction and path in our development of knowledge, point at which research design and methodology we should use, and define the theoretical and practical contributions our research is likely to generate. It is important to note that research questions can be understood in terms of different levels and with more or less precision and focus. In this book we see research questions not necessarily as very detailed questions or as specific objectives (close to testing an hypothesis). Instead, we regard research questions as setting the somewhat broader intellectual motive of a study, whether it is empirical and/or theoretical, that is, the rationale and direction of a study.

What makes a question a research question?

Although research questions are the core ingredient in all theory development, not all questions are research questions. A common criterion for what defines a research question is that it must be 'researchable' (White, 2009: 35) or, as Savin-Baden and Major (2012) have said, 'investigable'. Being researchable often means that research questions have to be formulated in such a way that they can be investigated scientifically and answered empirically. As White states: 'Not all questions are social science research questions ... other questions might be interesting to social scientists but cannot be answered using empirical evidence and so are not "researchable"' (2009: 35). Another common criterion is that a research question should not be too wide-ranging, but instead confined and focused. As Silverman suggests, research questions should be able to say 'a lot about a little' rather than 'a little about a lot' (2001: 5).

The above statements seem to assume that only empirical investigations require a research question. The recommendations are also directed at rather narrow empirical problems and investigations. However, research questions are equally central to projects that have a stronger theoretical and conceptual research focus. We can ask questions that do not necessarily call for a new, specific empirical inquiry to be conducted: many good research questions imply a thorough, critical, imaginative and synthesizing approach to the theories and empirical studies that already exist in a specific subject area. One could for example ask: 'What is the point of economic growth in countries that became "affluent" 50 years ago?'[1]. Or 'Why is leadership such a big research topic when people are more well-educated and claim to be more individualistic than ever?'[2] These kinds of questions call for an approach other than focused empirical inquiry. On the whole, this book aims to give a broader relevance to the theme of constructing and formulating research questions, and therefore does not limit itself to focused empirical inquiries such as those proposed by Silverman and others above.

Although being researchable and precise (or at least not too imprecise) is an important qualifier for a research question, at least in empirical research, this is not the only aspect to consider and doing so is typically not enough. Research questions should also be able to generate knowledge that matters to society and/or the larger professional practices under study (for example, education, health care: Adler and Hansen, 2012; Van De Ven, 2007). The point of research is of course not just to make it possible for academics to self-actualize or boost their narcissism and careers through seeing their names on publications, although one sometimes suspects that these kinds of motives do take the upper hand: research questions also need to have the potential to address the central problems in society in some way or another.

There is however often a tension between the criterion of mattering and the criteria of having researchable and precisely defined research questions, as well as between self-indulgent researchers and the interests of society. As Adler and Hansen note, many scholars tend to ask well-defined and neat (and as a consequence, sometime trivial) research questions 'rather than dedicating themselves to investigating large, messy, complex, controversial, and important societal issues' (2012: 5) that have the potential to make a difference to society. Research is often caught between rigor and relevance, and such debates remain evergreen in many fields. As we describe more fully in Chapter 7, a central reason for researchers' unwillingness to address complex and messy questions is their fear of deviating from what traditionally are seen as acceptable research questions and, thus, reducing their chances for publication, research funding and career progress.

While a research question should be considered in terms of its being researchable, precise and able to generate knowledge that matters, perhaps the main qualifier for a really good research question is that it can produce knowledge that has the potential to make a significant theoretical contribution. What a theoretical contribution consists of will be discussed more fully in Chapter 3. But broadly speaking it is possible to distinguish between two basic forms of theoretical contributions: to advance existing knowledge by incrementally adding to it or extending it in some significant way; and/or producing something more original and novel, for example, providing an alternative explanation or understanding of a specific subject matter (see also Corley and Gioia, 2011). As stated in Chapter 1, we are particularly interested in how to construct research questions from existing literature that will lead

---

[1] The term 'affluent' was coined by Galbraith in 1958.
[2] For an effort to illuminate these research questions see Alvesson (2013a).

to theoretical contributions which will challenge and differ from that existing literature in some significant way. This is because (as will be developed in Chapter 4) consensus-challenging knowledge is generally considered to be more interesting and to become more influential than consensus-confirming knowledge, which modifies and advances but rarely alters or adds significantly to existing knowledge within the scientific field.

But what characterizes research questions that may lead to consensus-challenging knowledge contributions? Such research questions are likely to be characterized by genuine *openness*. Being open creates unsettledness and indeterminacy, which are crucial for more original and revelatory knowledge to be developed. As Gadamer put it: 'To ask a question means to bring into the open. The openness of what is in question consists in the fact that the answer is not settled ... The significance of questioning consists in revealing the questionability of what is questioned' (1994: 363). Note here the double meaning of an 'open question' in the quote, namely, that it is characterized by both interrogating the subject matter *and* questioning what we already know about it. To be more specific, a genuinely open question addresses the subject matter anew and, at least temporarily, questions what we already know about it; in particular, the assumptions underlying our existing knowledge about it. Hence, innovative research questions open up and unsettle what we already 'know' about a subject. Such questions therefore have the potential to challenge our current understanding of the subject matter in some significant way and, thus, lead to the development of clearly novel knowledge.

It is important to note that some questions, which appear to be genuinely open, are in fact 'closed' questions in the sense that they do not open up the subject matter and instead preserve it. The prime example of closed questions is found in educational settings where the teacher pretends to ask students a genuinely open question but already has a ready-made answer. Another common example of closed questions is the kind of rhetorical questions often asked by politicians. Again, in such circumstances, the questioners will often know the answer but will want to temporarily unsettle their audience in some way or other. Unfortunately, similar kinds of more or less closed questions are frequently posed, deliberately or non-deliberately, within the social sciences, which to a large extent will tend to confirm what we already know (or believe we know). For example, the question 'How is gender being constructed among Spanish upper-class bisexuals?', implies that there are bisexuals constructing gender, and the question 'What are the attitudes to divorce in East Timor?', implies that there is something fairly uniform in East Timor and that people there have (fixed) attitudes about this issue. Yet another type of question that falls in between open and closed questions is what Gadamer calls 'slanted questions' (1994: 364). A question is slanted if it suggests openness but is posed in such a way that it does not, and therefore is not likely to, generate original and revelatory knowledge.

However, a research question can never be completely open: it is always limited by the specific perspective or horizon from which it is posed. In other words, a research question comes from somewhere; it is always constructed and formulated within a specific perspective that conceptualizes and determines the subject matter in a particular way. For example, questions about identity constructed and formulated within a psychological perspective are likely to differ from the questions about identity constructed and formulated within a sociological perspective. Similarly, questions about identity formulated within a specific theoretical perspective, such as trait psychology, are likely to differ from questions about identity formulated within a Foucauldian perspective. This means that questions open up the subject matter in particular ways while at the same time they limit the knowledge we can gain about the subject matter.

The fact that all research questions are constructed and formulated within certain frameworks, such as disciplinary, theoretical or methodological perspectives, but also within culturally taken-for-granted understandings, is important in two ways. First, it shows the importance of becoming aware of our own perspectives and how they affect the construction and formulation of our questions. This is because a particular perspective allows us to ask certain questions and thus develop particular knowledge and theories. Second, and most central in this book, it shows that a crucial element for developing more interesting and influential theory is to direct our attention not only towards constructing and formulating questions per se, but also towards the specific perspectives in which they are formulated and, in particular, the assumptions underlying those perspectives. Furthermore, to be able to formulate genuinely open questions, we may also need to deliberately challenge our own perspectives and cultural frameworks, at least temporarily. In other words, we need to be aware of the perspectives and their assumptions that govern the construction and formulations of our research questions. This is because the identification and challenging of assumptions underlying the perspectives and cultural 'truths' within which we are situated *precede* the construction and formulation of research questions. This is what the problematization methodology developed in Chapter 5 and exemplified in Chapter 6 will help us to do.

What types of research questions can be asked?

Although asking genuinely open questions is crucial for generating consensus-challenging knowledge contributions, it is also crucial to be able to distinguish and formulate different types of research questions. Several different types of research questions can be asked (Hesse-Biber and Leavy, 2011; Van de Ven, 2007; White, 2009). Dillon (1984) provides perhaps the most comprehensive review of different types of research questions. He identified 17 different types of research questions. It is, however, possible to group these 17 questions into four more overarching types, namely: descriptive; comparative; explanatory; and normative questions. A central observation made by Dillon is that these questions are to a large extent hierarchically related to each other in the sense that descriptive questions are the most basic, followed by comparative questions, and then explanatory and normative questions.

Descriptive questions, or what Dillon called first-order questions, are the most basic and aim to find out what makes up some phenomenon. Descriptive questions generate knowledge about what characterizes a phenomenon, such as its substance (for example, what it is), function (for example, what it does) and rationale (for example, why it has certain qualities). Examples of descriptive questions are 'What characterizes hyperactive people?' and 'How does student learning take place in an online environment?' These questions focus on the specific qualities that characterize hyperactive people and student learning, respectively.

The main purpose of *comparative*, or second-order, questions is to produce knowledge about the relations among phenomena, such as concomitance (for example, to what extent two phenomena are related to each other), equivalence (for example, to what extent two phenomena are similar to each other) and difference (for example, how two phenomena differ). An example of a comparative question is 'What similarities and differences, if any, exist between male and female receivers of social welfare?' As we can see, comparative questions entail and presuppose descriptive questions because they cannot be meaningfully answered before answering descriptive questions about what characterizes female and male welfare recipients.

Explanatory, or third-order, questions aim to generate knowledge about the contingent relations between phenomena and their attributes. Explanatory questions pursue correlation (for example, whether there is a contingent relation between specific attributes of two phenomena), conditionality (for example, if that correlation is conditioned by additional attributes) and causality (for example, if X produces a change in Y). Asking meaningful explanatory questions about contingent relations presupposes 'knowledge about comparative attributes' (Dillon, 1984: 331).

Normative questions aim to produce knowledge about how something should be done. Often normative questions ask what should be done in order to improve something, such as student learning, unemployment among young people or acceptance of homosexuality in groups known for their hostility towards such a sexual orientation. Again, as we can see, to be able to pose and answer normative questions requires answers from the previous types of questions.

The above typology highlights two key issues in constructing research questions. First, it highlights the importance of being aware that specific types of research questions generate specific kinds of knowledge. For example, if we want to generate knowledge about what makes up a phenomenon, we need to ask descriptive rather than explanatory questions. Second, and equally important, it shows that research questions are intimately related to each other in the sense that higher order questions entail lower-order questions. For example, to be able to ask comparative questions presupposes that we will first answer a set of descriptive questions.

It is important to note that a research question typically needs to be supplemented with a detailed and precise statement of *purpose* (Creswell, 1998; White, 2009), as a way to further sharpen the focus of a study. The purpose of a study postulates the researcher's intention with the study, that is, what the researcher wants to achieve with the study, such as describing, explaining or evaluating something (Ritchie, 2003; Savin-Baden and Major, 2012; White, 2009). We regard research questions as being broader and more general than purpose. This is because while purpose stipulates and clarifies what the researcher wants to achieve with a study, research questions frame the study in more significant ways. As stated above, research questions provide the overall direction and decide the path for the development of knowledge, as well as indicate what to look for, how to design the study, what methods should be used and what contributions the study can potentially make.

Where do research questions originate from?

A fourth major facet making up the context of constructing and formulating research questions is their origin. Research questions are not constructed and formulated in a vacuum but originate from the specific places from which the researcher gets their inspiration and ideas. While research questions are likely to come from a variety of places the four most common (and interrelated) are society (Silverman, 2001), personal experience (Easterby-Smith et al., 2008), existing scientific literature (White, 2009) and empirical material (Alvesson and Kärreman, 2011).

There are numerous issues in *society* that provide inspiration and ideas for research questions. For example, as reported in the media, managers and employees in our companies, policymakers and administrators in our various government bodies, teachers in our schools and health professionals in our hospitals constantly encounter problematic issues. Additionally, general trends in society, such as climate change, the global financial crisis, terrorism, major health issues, high unemployment, racism, changed migration patterns and the digitalization of the economy, can inspire questions. Therefore, watching news and documentaries on television, reading newspapers and specialist magazines, surfing the Internet, and more generally trying to stay in touch with what is going on in society and the world, can be important for generating an interesting research question. Using society as a source for constructing research questions is particularly critical to being able to generate research questions that matter.

Nonetheless, as Silverman (2001) and others have pointed out, it is crucial for several reasons to exercise caution when using broader society as the main source for generating research questions. It is not uncommon for managers, policymakers, trade unionists and politicians to drive their own specific agenda when pointing out some problematic issues in society. In other words, the issues communicated may appear to be genuine but can in reality be heavily fabricated or twisted as a way to push forward a certain agenda colored by various sectional interests, ideologies and political motives. And even if the issues raised are genuine they may be hard to turn into investigable research questions owing to their complexity and messiness. There are also often unrealistic expectations about the delivery of neat and reliable knowledge offering quick fixes. However, as we said before, this does not mean we should avoid broader social issues. Rather, it means we must carefully scrutinize to what extent it is possible to turn them into research questions, in particular into research questions that can make a real difference to society (Adler and Hansen, 2012).

Another common source of inspiration for generating research questions is *personal experience*. Through our personal experiences we are constantly exposed to various events that may function as sources in the construction and formulation of research questions. While there are several forms of personal experiences, three forms appear to be particularly central for generating research questions, namely work, life and study experience. Research interests may emerge from observations and the experience of being a teacher, having HIV/AIDS or having been in jail. Questions can also originate from a specific study experience, such as an inspiring course that triggered curiosity about a particular topic. However, our personal experiences may not only enable us to formulate specific research questions but also allow us function as filters that let in some aspects but leave out others and potential research questions. Personal experiences can also lead to fixed convictions and a belief that one already knows the answer to the question to be answered in the study.

Sometimes personal and research experiences will overlap, such as when people gradually develop new understandings, interests and questions during a project, which can provide input for the next research project. The output of one study can thus be the next study's input. For example, the output of a Master's thesis can provide input for a doctoral thesis. Similarly, a research project will often identify some unexamined issues and in many cases it is only at the end that the researcher recognizes the interesting new idea for study. Sometimes new research ideas are a matter of building directly on earlier reported results. But often there are other forms of outcome, such as the identification of questions that were outside the focus of the project and/or could not be answered, but provided a good starting point for later work. One could actually say that most good research leads to some (preliminary) answers and some new questions.

Although society and personal experience are important sources for developing research questions, *existing published studies and influential theory* are often the most common as well as the most important source for generating research questions. This is so for a variety of reasons. First, even if a research question originates elsewhere (either as a societal issue or from personal experience) a researcher needs to engage with existing literature to further elaborate the tentatively formulated research question. The researcher needs to review the existing literature to make sure that the formulated research question has not already been answered. Equally important, is that even if the formulated research question has not been addressed in the existing literature, this does not automatically mean that the researcher should pursue it. This is because there may be good reasons why it has not been addressed before, such as it may be unlikely to generate scientific knowledge. Existing studies and theory also help with finding the right framing and focus. How others have structured the field and what they managed to accomplish will be helpful for finding the right scope, sample and level of ambition in one's own study.

Second, the existing literature in itself provides a crucial source for generating research questions. Reviewing the existing literature in a particular area, such as higher education, family conflict or human aggression, enables us to tap into key debates and see which issues are central in the field, those that can function as important sources for constructing research questions. These questions need then to be further specified through a more targeted review of the existing literature as a way to see to what extent the question has been addressed, and how. In particular, the researcher needs to identify potential deficiencies and shortcomings in existing research that will enable him or her to develop questions that are likely to generate valuable, new knowledge. The critical scrutiny should not just focus on domain-specific issues or knowledge areas, but should also involve theoretical perspectives that the researcher is using or considering using, for example, psychoanalysis, symbolic interactionism or Marxism. A familiarity with critiques and debates is vital. Scrutiny may include both relevance/usefulness as well as possible problems and shortcomings in the theory, in general, or with a specific bearing on the subject matter of a study.

However, as White (2009) rightly points out, while the existing literature in an area can offer a rich source for constructing innovative research questions, it can also stifle creativity and innovation, as it tends to confine one's thinking. As the conclusion in Chapters 3 and 4 shows, generating research questions through building positively on existing studies leads mainly to the development of incremental knowledge contributions rather than more revelatory knowledge contributions. Therefore, the major part of this book addresses how to identify and challenge the assumptions underlying the existing literature and, based on doing so, formulate research questions that can lead to the development of more interesting and influential theories (see in particular Chapters 5 and 6).

Empirical material being produced in the research process can also function as a central source for research questions. In some cases, particularly in qualitative studies, being inductively oriented and open towards the views and meanings of those being studied may encourage revisions of the initial intention behind a study. Expectations may have been misleading. A researcher may want to study conflict and cooperation in teamwork and expect to find it, but then the actual research may show that the 'team' idea in this context is a management construction, that they are unaware of what actually goes on, and in fact workers tend to do the job fairly autonomously with rather limited contact with each other. Problems with access or unexpected changes in the object of study may also force revisions of the project.

Sometimes unexpected empirical material may have positive consequences, such as the researcher being able to generate more innovative research questions than those initially formulated. Often one is involved in specific empirical investigations about a topic when one sometimes suddenly 'sees' a potentially more interesting research question. (The case just mentioned about 'sham team work' could have started as a study of how workers hide work practices from management or, more generally, the existence and structuration of 'sham structures' in organizations.) This source may be more common for experienced researchers who are involved in various kind of empirical research. From the empirical material or the collection of empirical material, researchers may encounter issues that surprise them, deviate from expectations and so on. We discuss this further in Chapter 8.

There is of course always an initial research question but it is seldom set in stone, and even if it continues to guide the research to the end of the project, it is often to some extent influenced by the empirical setting and the gradual insights generated by the empirical results. In some cases empirical material may lead to more significant revisions. Although it is good in principle if the question precedes the search for answers, an interaction between questions and answers coupled with the search for a good research question during an exploratory research phase – and occasionally later – may be productive.

It is important to note that the formulation of research questions is often not a result from one specific source but one from an *interaction* between multiple sources, although the existing theory appears as the center of the interaction. This is because even if a research question originates from elsewhere, researchers still need to engage with the existing literature to make sure that it has not already been addressed or partly addressed and must then frame the research question in such a way that it will produce knowledge that makes a distinct theoretical contribution. In the interaction, the different sources can also temper each other's weaknesses. For example, we may be able to generate a promising research question from existing literature but then we also need to ask to what extent it matters to society. Similarly, if we are able to generate a research question based on some societal issues we need to consider to what extent it will add something of scientific value. If it does not do this, we will need either to reformulate the question or drop it. In some cases, in particular in qualitative research (often being more iterative), empirical material and findings may encourage re-readings of the literature and this can give rise to different ways of engaging with the literature in constructing and formulating a research question.

Factors that influence the construction and formulation of research questions

Regardless of their origin research questions are never constructed and formulated in isolation but always within the broader scientific fields and cultural frameworks in which the researcher is situated. As we will explain more fully in Chapter 7, scientific fields consist of a range of contextual factors and broader societal cultural traditions (for example, views on gender, authority, equality, community), which influence the construction and formulation of research questions in various ways.

One such contextual factor is *fashion and fads* in society and the social sciences. Popular topics often point to some critical problems in society or in a discipline that appear worthwhile for investigation. For example, fashionable topics in today's society are social media such as Twitter and Facebook, as well as the Internet more broadly, and how they affect our lives. Similarly, emotion, identity and workplace diversity are topics that are currently receiving a lot of attention in many disciplines.

Fashionable topics, like the above, tend to get a lot of attention in the media and in public debates and therefore appear to be important and worth studying. They have a propensity to direct and encourage researchers towards specific inquiry domains, and within them to construct and formulate specific research questions. However, just because an issue is fashionable does not mean that it is worth studying. The mass media often exaggerate trends and changes and like to emphasize drama. It is therefore vital not to automatically accept what is trendy but to critically scrutinize to what extent such topics may be worth studying. Often less fashionable but socially very important topics are persistent and it may be better to address them than look at what is considered to be new and hot. Another problem here is that what is viewed as a hot topic today may be cold tomorrow. A research contribution should ideally have some value over time. In addition, as it takes time to carry out research and to get it published, at least in scientific outlets, there is a risk that a trend-sensitive topic guiding a project may have lost its appeal when it is finally ready for publication, perhaps several years after the start of the project.

Another contextual factor that is likely to influence the formulation of research questions is the availability of *research funding*. Often funding bodies will have certain priority areas (sometimes influenced by what is in fashion), and if a research project falls inside such a priority area, it may increase the likelihood of getting funding. It is therefore not unusual that these priority areas influence how researchers construct and formulate their research questions in the sense that researchers will try to frame the research question so it seems to address a priority topic. *Journals* exercise a similar influence in the sense that they will have specific policies about what kind of research they publish and will often issue calls for papers on specific topics (to form special issues), which may influence the questions a researcher might ask. Often researchers will believe it is easier to get published in a special issue and then re-orient their work (or simply change some keywords and do some polishing) to try to get into it. However, while being opportunistic when it comes to applying for research funding and addressing a trendy topic may have some short-term benefits, such opportunism may be less positive in the long run and is therefore always a bit risky.

Another important contextual factor that tends to influence the formulation of research question is *other researchers*. It is common that more senior researchers within a school or department will influence the choice and formulations of research questions among doctoral students and more junior academics. For example, supervisors will tend to heavily influence their doctoral students' research questions. However peers who review research proposals and submitted papers may also influence how we construct and formulate our research questions. A highly interrelated contextual factor is researchers' *career prospects*. As mentioned above, many researchers tend to adjust their research questions to meet the criteria stipulated by funding bodies and journals, as a way to maximize the possibility of receiving research funding, getting published in good journals and, thus, climbing the ladder more quickly. Moreover, in order to increase the possibility of rising academically, many researchers will appear to avoid messy and complex questions and instead stick to doable – or even 'quick and dirty' – research tasks (Adler and Hansen, 2012). In particular, they seem to construct incremental and narrow research questions, which, as we will show in Chapters 3 and 4, are likely to lead to the development of less interesting and less influential knowledge contributions.

Another major influential factor is the researcher's specific *knowledge interest*. Habermas (1972) pointed out three basic forms of knowledge interest, namely, a technical, a practical-hermeneutic and an emancipatory knowledge interest, which guide scientific research and thus also the formulation of research questions.

A *technical* interest, which may be aligned with functionalist research, aims to develop knowledge of cause-and-effect relations through which control over natural and social conditions can be achieved. This approach is typically oriented towards discovering law-like patterns and offers instrumental knowledge that suggests how to accomplish the desired outcomes. For example, how we can improve institutional management, how to find out which teaching technologies are most effective and how to make interventions to prevent unwanted and deviant behavior. The *practical-hermeneutic* knowledge interest is more associated with interpretive scholarship. In contrast to a technical knowledge interest and its focus on prediction and control, a practical-hermeneutic knowledge interest emphasizes enriched understanding of human cultural experiences: how we communicate, generate and transform meaning. While interpretive scholars are fairly open with regard to how such knowledge can be used, they typically refrain from normative statements. The *emancipatory* knowledge interest comes from a more critical orientation often associated with various critical theory approaches. Here, attention is focused on power relations and revealing them in ways that can liberate the subject from various repressive relations that tend to constrain agency. This knowledge interest is about the critical examination of institutions, ideologies, interests and identities with the aim of encouraging critical insight, rethinking and liberation from, or resistance to, unnecessary social forms of domination. A closely related factor that also significantly influences the framing of research questions is the specific disciplinary, paradigmatic and methodological perspectives in which the researcher is situated, as discussed earlier.

The process of formulating research questions

Most research methodology textbooks conceptualize the process of formulating research questions as predominantly linear (Creswell, 1998; Savin-Baden and Major, 2012; White, 2009; Van de Ven, 2007). Although different authors distinguish the steps involved in the formulation of research questions in various ways, the formulation process is usually conceptualized as consisting of the following sequential steps. First, is to identify the domain or subject area with which we are interested, such as learning in higher education, domestic violence, youth unemployment and motivation. Then, we are advised to identify a specific topic within the domain or subject area, such as online learning in higher education or female violence among elderly couples. Thereafter, we should formulate a research problem in relationship to the chosen topic, with both a theoretical (for example, it is an area that has been largely overlooked) and practical (it is something that matters in society) motivation, that is, the rationale of the study. This is then often followed by the formulation of the purpose of the study, which clearly states what the study is about. Finally, we should specify the more precise direction of our research with a set of research questions.

While we partly agree with this description, we also think it is problematic as it leaves out several critical stages in the process of constructing and formulating research questions. First, we contend that the process is far more iterative and freely evolving than a linear progression allows. There appears to be, or at least ought to be, much more interaction between the sources from which research questions originate. Second, the existing literature seems to play a considerably more central role than the other sources in the formulation of innovative research questions. This is because even if a research question originates from another source the researcher still has to engage with the existing literature as a way to (1) generate a knowledge contribution, (2) achieve a firm base in what has been done previously, as well as drawing upon theoretical perspectives, and (3) make sure the construction and formulation of research questions do not only happen at the beginning of the research project but sometimes after an exploratory phase and occasionally even throughout the research. Sometimes the collection of empirical material and the initial interpretation of it can generate new insights that may require a reformulation of the research questions (Alvesson and Kärreman, 2011). As we highlight in Chapter 3, another crucial stage is the actual publication phase in which the research questions are finally formulated. It is, for example, not unusual for editors' and reviewers' comments to require a reformulation of research questions, as a way to further specify what kind of theoretical contribution the answers to the research questions have generated.

Conclusion

The aim of this chapter has been to situate our investigation of how researchers can construct research questions from the existing literature within the larger context of constructing and formulating research questions. We identified five major facets making up the context of generating research questions through the existing literature, namely: (1) the priority of questions/questioning in all knowledge development; (2) what makes a question a research question; (3) the major types of research questions that can be asked; (4) where do research questions originate from; and (5) the major contextual factors that influence the framing of research questions. Finally, we pointed to the evolving and iterative nature of generating research questions through existing literature. In summary, a consideration of the following issues seems particularly important when we are constructing and formulating research questions:

- Engagement and curiosity are important between strong commitment and openness, but be wary of conflict (as an engagement may lead to premature convictions and lock the project).
- Formulate questions that are open but also provide direction.
- Make certain of working with research questions, not just socially relevant or journalistic questions.
- Think through the knowledge interest, and what is the ultimate goal: instrumental value, enriched understanding, liberation through critical insight?
- Relate carefully and critically to the literature – do not just 'blindly' build positively on it.
- Funnel the research question – avoid too broad and vague questions.

- Beware of fashions and trends – research is a long-term oriented field.
- Be open to and reconsider what is to be done in the light of empirical findings.
- Be reflective about how broader contextual factors (for example, fashion, funding opportunities, journal policies and career prospects) may influence the construction and formulation of research questions.

In Chapters 3 and 4 that follow, we narrow our focus and specifically investigate the ways social science researchers construct and formulate research questions from the existing literature, and to what extent these ways are likely to result in the development of more interesting and influential theories.

3

GAP-SPOTTING: THE PREVALENT WAY OF CONSTRUCTING RESEARCH QUESTIONS IN SOCIAL SCIENCE

In Chapter 2, we discussed the larger context of constructing and formulating research questions. The aim of this chapter is to investigate more specifically how researchers within the social sciences construct their research questions in relation to the existing literature. We will do so by reviewing a number of research texts in management, sociology, psychology and education. We will also refer to a few studies in other areas but believe that these four give a representative view of the current state of research in the social sciences. We do, however, recognize variations between and within disciplines as well as between various regions of the world. For example, what appears in leading international journals published in the USA is likely to be different from what is published in research books in Scandinavia. While we would acknowledge the presence of such variations and others, our interest is in internationally salient studies published in journals and we will not attempt to cover all national variations in research, nor those between different types of research outlets.

Our findings suggest that the most common way of producing research questions is to spot various gaps in the existing literature, such as an overlooked area, and based on that to formulate specific research questions. Gap-spotting is of course not something absolute but varies in both scope and complexity: from incrementally extending an established theory to identifying more significant gaps in the existing literature. We will summarize the basic gap-spotting modes and their specific versions in a typology of gap-spotting research.

How researchers construct research questions from the existing literature

By examining how researchers construct their research questions from the existing literature we are, in one sense, unable to say anything definite about how researchers 'really' arrive at their research questions. It is a complex issue, involving a variety of interacting processes and influencing elements, such as timing, chance, actively seeking exposure to different views and being immersed in the literature, as well as paradigmatic, social and cultural conditions. As was described in Chapter 2, in some instances, fashion and opportunism may also influence the research conducted. For example, people may become aware of a special issue of a journal on a fashionable topic or a conference on a specific theme and will therefore try to revise the framing and formulation of their research question to fit into the theme. Empirical experiences are also often crucial. We may have started in a particular way but, as the research evolves, gradually have changed our understanding of the research object. Therefore we may revise the research question many times between the beginning of a project and publication.

However, we believe that research texts indicate something about how researchers develop research questions from existing theory and, under all circumstances, highlight the social norms and methodological rules that are likely to influence how they construct their research questions and underpin their claim to make a contribution to the scientific field, which is highly important in itself. We would even claim that apart from those arguably rare cases where a researcher has a clear and fixed research question from the very start and keeps to this even in the published research report, there will inevitably be revisions and modifications of how that researcher defines his or her project and its research question. Very few researchers will stop reading having covered sufficient literature to get started. All the literature consumed during the research process, including new literature read after receiving comments from reviewers pointing at shortcomings in the literature review and new angles to be considered, may influence the construction of the research question in relation to the available literature. Such changes are of course most salient in qualitative studies and conceptual papers, which tend to be more open than hypothesis-testing studies. In the former, as well as in studies where the author is building on various ideas that gradually have been developed and/or is inspired by several empirical studies he or she has conducted over the years, there is seldom any clear starting point for the construction of the research question.

This is not to say that there are no examples of studies where a research question produced at an early stage strictly guides the research project until the study appears in print. One may assume that it would be easier to produce a coherent and rigorous paper if there is no significant discrepancy between the early stages (or early drafts of publications) and the published versions of research, at least not a significant one. Making drastic changes to the research question late in the research process may lead to inconsistencies in the project as a whole and in the text approaching publication. In some cases, the formulated research question is likely to be very similar to the ideas and purposes that inspired the researcher at earlier stages in the research process. In other cases, the research question presented in the published text may bear a stronger relationship to considerations of how to craft a persuasive text (rhetoric) and thus differ from the researcher's ambitions and thoughts in the initial stages of the research process.

However, whether the research process is characterized by a gradually changing research question or an intact from-the-start question, a discrepancy between the 'real' initial research question and the one espoused in a published text may not be particularly important or interesting. Our argument here is that the vital element is not whether there is variation in the various 'real' research questions guiding the research over time, or whether there is consistency between stages. Rather, the only research question of real interest, when it comes to generating high-impact research, is the one espoused in the published text guiding the actual knowledge contribution. In other words, *it is in the crafting of the research text that the final research question is constructed, which is the one that specifies the actual contribution of the study*. Our interest is therefore in the research questions leading to research results, as communicated to the research community, and not in trying to trace the various moves of the researcher over time.

Hence, by studying research texts, we do not make strong claims about what actually influenced the emergence of the research question during the first stages of the research process. Instead, what we offer is an inquiry into the relationship between literature in a field and the (formulated) research question guiding the delivery of the (final) results – as expressed in the scientific text. This means that any strong distinction between what 'really' guided the researcher and 'pure' rhetoric is of less relevance here. Rather than the 'real' or the 'presented' research question, we are interested in the constructed research question – the one presented in the publication and governing the actual contribution. More cautiously by investigating research publications, and for the benefit of concerned readers feeling that there is a significant gap between 'real' and 'expressed' research questions, we can at least say something about the social norms and methodological rules that are likely to influence how researchers construct their research questions from the existing literature. These norms are likely to have 'truth-creating' effects: how researchers present their ways of formulating research questions will influence other researchers and frame the scientific field.

Investigating scientific texts in order to understand the research process has also been longstanding common practice within the sociology of science (Davis, 1971, 1986; Golden-Biddle and Azuma, 2010; Knorr-Cetina, 1981; Latour and Woolgar, 1979). The research that probably comes closest to the study reported here in this chapter is Locke and Golden-Biddle's (1997) and Golden-Biddle and Locke's (2007) studies of how researchers create an opportunity for contributing to scholarly journals.

According to Locke and Golden-Biddle's study, establishing opportunities to contribute includes two main processes, namely, structuring intertextual coherence and problematization. In structuring an intertextual field, the researcher tries to bring together existing studies into a context for contribution 'that reflects the consensus of previous work' by using a range of textual strategies (1997: 1029). They identified three textual strategies for connecting existing studies into a context for contribution: synthesized coherence, progressive coherence and non-coherence. When using *synthesized coherence*, researchers 'cite and draw connections between works and investigative streams not typically cited together to suggest the existence of underdeveloped research areas' (1997: 1030). In contrast, *progressive coherence* is used to establish a context for contribution characterized by a network of studies that are linked by 'shared theoretical perspectives and methods working on research programs that have advanced over time' (1997: 1030). Finally, *non-coherence* is used to describe a common research field marred by disagreement.

In the second process, the researcher 'problematizes' the established context of a contribution as being deficient in some way in order to open up 'opportunities for advancing knowledge about topics of investigative concern' (1997: 1029). According to Locke and Golden-Biddle, almost half of the studies used an *incompleteness* strategy to construct an opportunity to contribute by claiming that existing literature was incomplete in some way or another, and that the researcher's own study would be able to advance it. Another common way was to critique existing literature for being *inadequate* in some significant way. Here, it is claimed that the prior literature has overlooked an important perspective, which would have had the potential to further our understanding of the subject matter. A third and noticeably more uncommon way of questioning existing theory was to claim that it was *incommensurate*. Advocates of these (eight) studies argued that the existing literature not only neglected certain perspectives but also misguided the way knowledge was produced about the subject matter in question. The opportunity to contribute then is to provide a superior perspective that will correct the faulty existing literature. These findings have also been confirmed more recently in other research areas, such as information systems (Barrett and Walsham, 2004), marketing (Johnson, 2003) and strategy as practice (Golden-Biddle and Azuma, 2010).

Constructing research questions and creating an opportunity to contribute are fairly close in the sense that there is a created space in which to contribute points to a specific question, and vice versa. It is therefore likely that Locke and Golden-Biddle's (1997) analysis reveals key aspects of how researchers construct research questions from the existing literature in research texts. For example, the strategies used to create an opportunity to contribute indicate that a central component in the ways researchers construct research questions is to review the existing literature in order to find some deficiency in it (is it incomplete, inadequate, or even incommensurate?) and based on that, to motivate and specify their particular research questions. However, although their study provides valuable insights and conceptualizations of how researchers construct research questions from the existing literature, their primary aim was not to articulate how researchers arrived at their research questions and, even less, to investigate which routes were likely to lead to the development of interesting theories.

Therefore, the study reported in this chapter both extends and differs from Locke and Golden-Biddle's work in three notable ways. First, our study specifically investigates and proposes a distinct typology for how researchers construct research questions from the existing literature, with a particular focus on ways that are likely to lead to interesting and influential theories. Second, as outlined below, we cover a much broader set of journals, studying a mix of qualitative and quantitative studies, and investigating a more recent sample of research texts, namely those published between 2003 and 2011. Perhaps the increasing popularity of 'skeptical' approaches, such as poststructuralism and critical studies, has modified the assessment made by Locke and Golden-Biddle?

Method and research design

In order to identify how management researchers construct research questions from the existing literature, we reviewed eight different issues from the following leading US and European management and organization journals: *Administrative Science Quarterly*, *Journal of Management Studies*, *Organization Studies* and *Organization*. These journals' relevance is not limited to understanding what people do in business schools and management departments as (apart from the *Journal of Management Studies*) they are interdisciplinary and include articles from researchers in fields such as sociology, education, psychology, political science, information systems, and so on. We selected two issues from each journal from the period 2003–2005 and avoided special issues. The main reasons for choosing these journals were that they are all considered to be premier outlets for leading edge management and organization research, they represent a fairly good spread when it comes to the kind of research they publish, and they complement Locke and Golden-Biddle's study in important ways.

Despite their interdisciplinary nature, there is of course the possibility that the selected journals bear the imprints of specific field characteristics associated with publishing in organization studies. In order to situate our study in the social sciences more broadly we therefore also reviewed eight recent issues from leading US and European journals in sociology, psychology and education: the *American Journal of Sociology*, *Sociology*, *Psychological Science*, the *Journal of Applied Psychology*, the *American Educational Research Journal* and *Learning and Instruction*. The total number of articles reviewed amounted to 119 (52 management/organization articles, 23 psychology articles, 21 sociology articles and 23 education articles). About one-half of the authors were from North America and those remaining from the rest of the world (mainly from the UK). When reading and assessing these journals we reached saturation after about 100 articles were reviewed, that is, despite reviewing more articles from each discipline we did not identify any new ways of constructing research questions. As the basic patterns from our initial study were confirmed, we saw little point in further exploration.

Similar to Locke and Golden-Biddle (1997) and others (Bazerman, 1993; Golden-Biddle and Azuma, 2010), although we examined the entire articles, we concentrated on the first part of the articles (from the introduction to the method section), as it was there that the researchers most clearly expressed their ways of constructing research questions from the existing literature. In particular, we carefully read the selected research texts and looked for key statements where the authors signaled how they had constructed their research questions from earlier research and theory.

In the subsequent analysis we searched for the meaning underlying the logic behind the ways of constructing research questions rather than using a detailed coding, as in grounded theory. Generally, the logic was often explicitly stated in the research texts. For instance, Musson and Tietze formulated their research question by saying that they would 'address this gap' in the literature (2004: 1301), as did Hammer et al. by saying they would 'address these gaps in work-family intervention research' (2011: 135). Similarly, Westphal and Khanna argued that they would 'extend this literature' in a specific way (2003: 363), while Jones et al. constructed their research question by claiming that there had been 'little empirical research' (2010: 104) in the focused area. Hence, in most cases the different modes of constructing research questions described below suggested themselves more or less directly from the selected research texts.

A typology of how researchers construct research questions from the existing literature

The most dominant way of constructing research questions in our empirical material was *gap-spotting*. Researchers reviewed the existing literature with the aim of spotting gaps in the literature and based on doing so formulated specific research questions. We identified three basic modes of gap-spotting, namely, confusion, neglect and application spotting. We were also able to distinguish specific versions of spotting gaps within each basic gap-spotting mode. The basic gap-spotting modes and their specific versions are summarized in Table 3.1 and further elaborated on below.[1]

Table 3.1 Basic modes of gap-spotting and their specific versions

Basic gap-spotting modes	Specific versions of basic gap-spotting modes
Confusion spotting	Competing explanations
Neglect spotting	Overlooked area
	Under-researched
	Lack of empirical support
	Lacking a specific aspect
Application spotting	Extending and complementing existing literature

Confusion spotting

The main focus in this way of constructing research questions is to spot some kind of confusion in the existing literature. Previous research on the topic exists, but the available evidence is mixed and contradictory. The research question aims to sort out the identified confusion in the literature and explain it. The main version of this mode of constructing research questions was to search for *competing explanations* in the existing literature.

Anderson and Reeb's (2004) study of board composition can be seen as a typical representative of this particular version within the management literature. According to them, it is widely recognized in the corporate governance

---

[1] See Appendix 1 for an extended table in which all the reviewed journal articles are classified according to the various gap-spotting versions identified.

literature that large shareholders, such as founding families, tend to exploit smaller shareholders' portion of a firm's wealth. There is also a fairly widespread belief that independent directors are in a position to reduce the above conflict. There are, however, competing explanations for this. According to agency theory, independent directors can defend smaller shareholders' interests by executing control over founding families' tendency to exploit a firm's wealth at a cost to small shareholders. Conversely, stewardship theory claims that because founding families identify themselves closely with their firms, they tend to regard a firm's health 'as an extension of their own well-being' (Anderson and Reeb, 2004: 211) and are therefore keen to bring in independent directors who can advise on ways to keep their firms fit and profitable. Anderson and Reeb try to 'disentangle these competing theories – agency theory and stewardship – by examining the influence of affiliated directors … and by examining the manner in which independent directors gain their board seats amongst family and non-family firms' (2004: 211).

Another example of using competing explanations in the literature to construct research questions is Gibbons's study of how social networks influence professional values. In her review of the literature, she finds strong evidence 'that social systems tend toward consensus in values among their members at the same time as there are ample of studies that report "discrepancies among individuals" values in organizations' (2004: 238). According to Gibbons, this leads to two related questions. 'First, which informal social forces support convergence and which foster divergence from established professional values? Second, as professional values change, how does this influence existing social networks?' (2004: 238).

Similarly, Liu et al. (2010) utilized the competing explanation route to construct their research questions about the sudden increase in autism during the 1990s in the USA. According to the authors, although several hundred studies have been carried out, those studies have generated competing accounts so we still do not know why the sudden increase in autism happened. The aim of their study is therefore to bring clarity about what caused the increase in autism 'by disentangling these competing accounts', that is, if the sudden increase was caused by 'social influence, toxicological change, or viral transmission … In this article, we design a data structure and a series of critical tests to disentangle these explanations' (2010: 1390).

In constructing the research questions in their study about people's perception of modern arts, Hawley-Dolan and Winners (2011) also followed the competing explanation route. According to them, many laypeople argue that people cannot really distinguish paintings made by professional artists from paintings made by preschoolers and animals, such as monkeys and elephants. This claim has also found some support among scholars. However, other studies suggest that people in fact can distinguish a painting made by a professional artist from 'scribbles' created by a preschooler or an animal. Hawley-Dolan and Winners therefore set out to resolve these competing claims by formulating their research question as follows: 'Either abstract art really is indistinguishable from the markings of the unskilled or these confusions are more apparent than real' (2011: 435). (For the reader curious about the results, and especially those fond of abstract art and perhaps worried about the outcome of the study, we should add – reassuringly – that the findings suggest that it is possible to distinguish the work of professional artists from the work of small children or monkeys.)

Likewise, Papay (2011) used the competing explanation route to construct his research question in a study of so-called value-added models for evaluating teacher performance. He begins by pointing out that during the last two decades both scholars and practitioners have 'increasingly adopted value-added methods to evaluate student, teacher, and school performance'. However, the research community remains divided over the ultimate usefulness of value-added estimates for policy. In particular, they are divided over to what extent value-added models are valid and reliable. According to Papay, 'some argue that the methodologies support causal claims that specific teachers increase student achievement; as such, compensation and accountability policies based on these estimates are justified ... others, however, assert that the many assumptions underlying these models make such claims tenuous at best' (2011: 164). The aim of his study was therefore to try to settle this division among educational scholars.

Neglect spotting

Spotting something neglected in the existing literature is the most common mode of constructing research questions in our sample. Researchers using this strategy try to identify a topic or an area where no (good) research has been carried out. There is virgin territory – a blank area on the knowledge map – that produces an imperative for the alert scholar to develop knowledge about the neglected area(s) and, thus, being able to add something to the existing literature in question. It is possible to distinguish four specific *versions* of neglect spotting, namely, spotting an overlooked area, an under-researched area, a lack of empirical support and a lack of specific aspects that need to be added to make the existing literature more complete.

The most common version of neglect spotting was to search for areas in existing literature that had been *overlooked* despite a wealth of studies. This is evident in Luke's study of how migrants who form non-family ties in many urban destinations compete with 'origin families for a share of remittances' (2010: 1436). She points out that prevalent research has focused on how migration is used as a household strategy for generating income for the family from which the migrant originates. She then goes on to point out that while we know a great deal about migration remittance behavior towards origin families, '[r]emarkably absent from the literature on remittance behavior is the study of new *non-familial* ties that migrants forge in the destination and the benefits and costs associated with these exchange relationships' (2010: 1436). The spotted overlooked area enables her to construct a research question that addresses an important gap in the migration literature.

Similar, Judge and Cable (2011) applied the overlooked version to construct research questions in their study of the extent to which body size is correlated with wage pay. They claim that while some economists have studied 'wage penalties applied to obesity' they 'are not aware of any study in the organizational behavior literature that has examined the weight – earnings relationship or gender differences therein' (2011: 95), that is, an overlooked area, and this is what they are going to investigate in their study.

Spotting overlooked areas as a way of constructing research questions was also used by Kopp and Mandl (2011) in their study of learners' argumentation justification. The researchers review the literature and claim that it has 'mainly measured the individual's ability to justify arguments' (2011: 637). They then point out 'there is almost no research regarding the collaborative justification of arguments' (2011: 637). The aim of their study is therefore to investigate and measure both collaborative and individual argumentation justification.

Searching for *under-researched* areas in existing literature is another common version of neglect spotting. In contrast to the overlooked type, the under-researched route acknowledges that some research has been carried out about a particular topic, but claims that further studies are needed to better understand and explain it. A good representative of this route is Corley and Gioia's (2004) study of ambiguity in organizational identity change in corporate spin-offs. They review the organizational change literature and conclude that a strong bias exists in the literature toward empirical examinations of additive types of changes, such as mergers and assimilations. Much less attention has been paid to studying subtractive changes such as downsizing or spin-offs. They also found that 'although past research has provided insight into why organizational identities change … it has not provided adequate insight into *how* organizational identity change can occur' (2004: 174, emphasis in original). Thus, they set out to study how organizational identity changes occur in spin-off organizations.

Fox (2011) used the under-researched version to construct a research question about boundary objects and technology adoption. In his literature review he points out that while a growing body of research has investigated how boundary objects can 'enhance the capacity of an idea, theory or practice to translate across culturally defined boundaries, for example, between communities of knowledge or practice… it remains sociologically under-theorized' (2011: 70). In particular, he constructs his research question by claiming that while existing literature raises important questions about 'which objects might perform such functions … more needs to be known about how they function and what makes them effective' (2011: 73).

Likewise, O'Connor et al. (2011) constructed their research question by spotting an under-researched area. According to them, there is an extensive body of research, which shows 'that teacher-child relationships play an important role in children's socio-emotional and behavioral development' (2011: 125). However, the literature review suggests that 'our understanding of teacher-child relationships and children's behavior problems in elementary school remains limited as previous research has been mostly cross-sectional, examining associations between the quality of early teacher-child relationships and the extent of later behavior problems, and few studies have considered the multiple systems within which children develop' (2011: 127). Their study will address this neglected area in the literature.

A similar but different version of neglect spotting is to search for areas in existing literature that *lack empirical support*. For example, in reviewing the literature on organizational learning, Dyck et al. (2005) came to the conclusion that most of the theoretical concepts and models that were supposed to capture the nature of organizational learning have had little empirical support. This led them to study the extent to which current key concepts and models of organizational learning have been empirically supported. In a similar vein, Richler et al. constructed their research question by pointing out that although the concept of holistic processing plays a pivotal role in face-recognition research, 'holistic processing and face-recognition ability have never been linked empirically' (2011: 464). Likewise, Jadallah et al. (2011) point out in their literature review about scaffolding methods (i.e. ways of assisting students to solve a problem that they couldn't otherwise have done), that there is a lack of empirical consensus about what characterizes successful scaffolding methods. The aim of their study is therefore 'to provide more specificity and greater empirical grounding for scaffolding methods that can be successfully employed during classroom discussion' (2011: 197).

The most incremental way of neglect spotting was to search for *a lack of specific aspects* in existing literature. This version of neglect spotting differs from the others, as it appears to focus on smaller gaps in the existing literature. Interestingly, this version of neglect spotting was only found within psychology. For example, Liu et al. (2011) studied to what extent people's beliefs in global warming were malleable/influenced by the current weather of the day, that is, if it was a cool or hot day when they were asked about their beliefs. Therefore, as a way of adding to existing literature on people's beliefs in global warming they focused on 'relative temperature deviation rather than absolute temperature deviation, which the previous studies examined' (2011: 455).

Application spotting

Spotting a new application in the existing literature is a third basic mode of constructing research questions. It involves searching mainly for a shortage of a particular theory or perspective in a specific area of research. The research task is to provide an alternative perspective to further understanding of the particular subject matter in question. Typically, advocates of application spotting claim that a specific body of literature needs to be *extended* or *complemented* in some way or another. An example of this version can be found in Watson's (2004) study 'HRM and critical social science analysis'. He reviewed the existing HRM (human resource management, previously known as personnel administration) literature and concluded that it lacked a more critical perspective. Too much HRM literature is prescriptive and normative. In order to address this inadequacy, Watson's research task was to introduce a critical theory perspective into current HRM literature.

Application spotting was absent in psychology and rare in education but quite common in the sociology articles. For example, Oliver and O'Reilly (2010) reviewed the literature on lifestyle migration and noted a steady decline in including the notion of class in such studies. As a way to rectify this problem, the authors proposed and elaborated a Bourdieusian perspective, which according to the authors 'offers a fresh perspective to migration studies' (2010: 50). Similarly, Taylor applies application spotting in generating his research question about 'the role and function of emotion management in an animal shelter' (2010: 85). He is critical of traditional approaches to animal shelter emotion management, which according to Taylor, privileges the researchers. As an alternative perspective he proposes a performative perspective, which enables an investigation of animal shelter emotion management in situ. In education, Russell constructed her research question about how educational systems evolve over time using kindergartens as an example by offering 'an alternate yet complementary perspective, which emphasizes how popular conceptions of what constitutes a kindergarten education may have shifted' (2011: 237).

Combinations

While many of the studies reviewed emphasize one major way of constructing research questions, *combinations* of different gap-spotting modes are not uncommon. For example, in constructing their research question, Schultze and Stabell (2004) adopted an approach that was partly confusion spotting, and partly application spotting. Their aim was to 'explore the contradictory, double-edged nature of knowledge by developing a theory-informed framework that highlights different assumptions about knowledge and its management' (2004: 550). The framework draws upon the paradigm framework of Burrell and Morgan (1979) and the revision of this by Deetz (1996).

Combining different gap-spotting modes was also evident in the other fields investigated. For instance, Daly and Finnigan (2011) constructed their research questions by spotting a lack of empirical work and an overlooked area in a specific field of education. In their review they identified that 'limited empirical work has examined the underlying social networks between school and district leader' and at the same time spotted that 'this literature frequently overlook[s] that organizational reform efforts are socially constructed' (2011: 39). Similarly, in psychology Le et al. (2011) generated their research question by spotting a lack of empirical work and a confusion in existing literature within a specific field in psychology. An example of combination within the sociological field is Hook's (2010) study of gender inequality in household work in which she constructs her research question by spotting an underresearched area together with confusion spotting in terms of competing explanations.

Some qualifying comments: within and beyond gap-spotting

From the above analysis we can conclude that gap-spotting is by far the most common way of constructing research questions within the social sciences (at least within the fields studied). However, before critically evaluating to what extent gap-spotting research is likely to lead to interesting and influential theories it is necessary to qualify this picture of existing ways of generating research questions. Researchers can arrive at or formulate their research questions in ways other than gap-spotting. Two such routes are critical confrontation and a new idea. They sometimes overlap or co-exist with gap-spotting and are sometimes put into action without any argumentation about gap-filling. In addition, there are also sometimes elements of problematization involved in the gap-spotting strategies we identified to offer the major rationale behind a specific objective for a research article. Such elements often consist of earlier critical questioning and ways of revising a specific theory. Below, we first describe critical confrontation and new idea as complementary but also independent strategies for generating research questions. Thereafter, we point at supplementing strategies that are sometimes involved in gap-spotting strategies.

Critical confrontation

Here, the researcher criticizes a theory or a field based on the identification of some shortcomings. The critical confrontation may take the form of application spotting, such as when a particular area lacks a critical perspective. This was, for example, evident in the sociologist Sayer's (2011) use of application spotting to generate a research question. He confronted the dominant explanations that class inequalities are primarily rooted in a symbolic domination by claiming it is partly inadequate. This is because it does not take into account how embodied disposition and practice play a crucial role in explaining class inequalities. He then went on to offer a new perspective that combines Bourdieu's theory of practice and the theory of contributive justice as a way to rectify the inadequacy in existing explanations.

Critical reviews may also be framed in more confrontational ways worthy of their own category (for example, as different from application spotting). Often the critique may focus on rather narrow topics, such as faulty methods or errors in reasoning. One example is Yukl's (1999) critical examination of research on transformational leadership. His examination offers a critique of various theoretical claims without more than marginally considering the assumptions behind these. Sometimes basic assumptions can also be targeted, as is often the case with feminist, critical theory and poststructuralist writings. Typically the critical confrontation takes the form of programmatic problematization, as referred to in Chapter 1. It falls outside gap-spotting, but does not qualify as 'genuine' problematization as it does not deliberately focus on challenging the assumptions underlying an existing theory.

New idea

This simply means that the author emphasizes a new idea. The author claims innovation without reference to a literature review of what has not already been studied. This means sidestepping both building on and challenging existing studies. It calls for original thinking and a high level of self-confidence. However, this approach is not so common in today's social science, which is perhaps to be expected as so much has already been said. We did not find any clear examples in the fields investigated in our sample. Nevertheless, this does not mean that examples are non-existent. Classical work often exhibits this quality, more or less involving a strong challenge to existing assumptions, but this is not necessarily framed as such – and therefore different from what we mean by problematization.

Some more 'classics' that offer good examples are Geertz's (1973) view of culture and Lasch's (1978) idea of the culture of narcissism. One more recent example is Gabriel (2005), who suggests the glass cage and the glass palace as new metaphors for organizations. He relates these metaphors to Weber and many others, but not in a way that identifies some un-researched terrain within Weber-inspired studies, nor as a problematization of the iron cage theory or literature. Originality in this sense sidesteps the issue of problematization or other explicit routes to research questions. There is often an implicit reference to gap-spotting. But while gap-spotting typically identifies a narrow area that has not been (sufficiently) studied, the new idea approach claims a broader, more conceptual contribution.

Ingredients of problematization in the framework drawn upon in gap-spotting

Apart from directly expressing critical confrontation or proposing a new idea, much work draws upon earlier critical scrutiny and suggested revisions of theories, where there may be more or fewer strongly evident elements of problematization. A gap-spotting study can thus show its origin in the outcomes of earlier problematization. For example, Heijes, an anthropologist, refers to Hofstede's (1980) well-known work on the nature and consequences of national cultures, and then reviews the extensive critique of 'the supposed cohesiveness and causality of the culture concept' (2011: 654). The critique of course involves suggestions of carrying out research in another way, based on alternative starting points. Heijes then associates himself with the critics and suggests a view on culture as 'dynamic and co-created in dialogue', that is, the importance of considering the interplay between power (associated with hierarchical position) and culture. Based on this premise he arrives at his research question, involving the ambition to 'expand on this interaction between culture and power and discuss the role of power and power differences in cross-cultural perception' (2011: 655). This is a clear example of gap-spotting, building on earlier work involving critique and problematization, but reproducing the assumptions of the preceding work.

Another example, exhibiting slightly more of problematization, although not so explicitly framed as such, is Sauder and Espeland's (2009) study of the effects of rankings on US law schools. They draw upon institutional theory and Foucault to invoke the observation that the law schools failed to develop legitimizing structures that protected their actual practice from the impact of the rankings. The development of legitimizing structures is otherwise claimed by institutional theory, at least some dominant versions of it (Meyer and Rowan, 1977), arguing that organizations develop legitimizing structures that are decoupled from actual practice and that the latter is 'saved' from the pressure to be transformed. This is called buffering. However, the US law schools were unsuccessful in such operations and the ranking regime had far-reaching effects on the decisions taken and operations in the schools, despite their strong hostility towards the rankings. These empirical observations are connected with institutional theory and there is an element of empirically driven problematization in the research question.

In the case of Sauder and Espeland there is no deeper investigation of the assumptions of institutional theory and their major theoretical inspiration is Foucault, who is quite straightforwardly applied: 'this article explains the value of Michel Foucault's concept of discipline for understanding why these organizations are unable to buffer themselves from this new institutional pressure' (2009: 64). The paper is interesting as its illustrates how there are some elements of problematization, or at least use of a case deviating from an important theoretical source of inspiration (institutional theory), while at the same time it is mainly guided by the application of Foucault's theory. A further example is Penfold-Mounce et al.'s (2011) study that illustrates how the television program *The Wire*'s investigation of various sociological themes can function as a great resource for sociological imagination and, thus, new and innovative research questions.

We can thus point to various complexities and variations in exactly how researchers formulate their research questions in relationship to the literature, including how empirical observations and other issues become involved. This should however not lead us away from our core finding in this chapter, namely that *the great majority of contemporary researchers in many social science fields primarily use gap-spotting as their rationale for constructing their research questions.*

Conclusion

In this chapter we have investigated the ways in which contemporary researchers construct research questions from the existing literature. It is clear that gap-spotting is the dominant way of developing research questions from existing literature, at least in journal articles in many social science disciplines. It is by looking for 'gaps' – either a lack of studies or shortage in the delivery of conclusive results in the existing literature – that research questions are constructed. Within the overall category of gap-spotting, we identified three basic versions, namely, confusion, neglect and application spotting. In the next chapter we critically discuss the limitations and problems of gap-spotting research: in particular to what extent gap-spotting research is likely to lead to the development of interesting and influential theories.

4

A CRITICAL EVALUATION OF GAP-SPOTTING RESEARCH: DOES IT LEAD TO INTERESTING THEORIES?

From the analysis in the previous chapter we can conclude that gap-spotting is by far the most common method researchers employ in constructing research questions within the social sciences (at least in management, education, psychology, sociology). The aim of this chapter is to evaluate critically the extent to which generating research questions through gap-spotting is likely to lead to the development of interesting and influential theories. We begin by reviewing and discussing the theories of interestingness, that is, the bodies of literature that investigate what makes a theory interesting and influential. In the light of the theories of interestingness, we critically evaluate to what extent gap-spotting is likely to lead to high-impact research. Finally, we reflect on whether something 'interesting' perhaps goes on behind the research questions appearing in research publications.

What makes a theory interesting and Influential?

The central question in this chapter is to what extent gap-spotting is likely to facilitate the development of interesting and influential theories. In order to answer that question adequately we need, first, to understand what makes a theory interesting, that is, how it attracts attention from other researchers and, thus, becomes influential. Although different people may find different studies and theories interesting, interestingness is hardly just a matter of idiosyncratic opinion. As stated in Chapter 1, collectively held assessments of what counts as interesting research are much more prevalent than purely subjective views, even though the collective can be restricted to a sub-community rather than an entire field, such as school research within education.

The hallmark of a 'good' theory has been that it is truthful to its subject matter and derived from rigorous research. But as the sociologist Davis (1971) showed in his seminal work, what makes a theory notable, and sometimes even famous (Davis, 1986), is not only that it is seen as true but also, and more importantly, that it is seen as challenging the assumptions underlying existing theories in some significant way. As Davis expressed it, 'the social researcher who wants to be certain that he [sic] will produce an *interesting* theory about his subject must first familiarize himself with what his audience already assumes to be true about his subject, before he can even begin to generate a proposition which, in denying their assumption, will attract their attention' (1971: 337, emphasis in original).

Although many theorists have described how a theory by challenging assumptions can be made more interesting, Davis (1971, 1986, 1999) has discussed this most fully. It can therefore be worthwhile looking into his findings in more detail to better understand how challenging assumptions can make a theory interesting and thereby influential. In his seminal article 'That's interesting!' Davis (1971) examined what makes a particular theory receive considerable attention and thus become more influential than others. He specifically looked at highly influential and famous theories in the social sciences, and examined what these influential theories had in common, that is, what made them interesting and worth paying attention to relative to other theories.

As pointed out above, the defining factor for a theory to be seen as interesting and influential is that it challenges some of the routinely taken-for-granted assumptions about an audience's everyday life, that is, what seems to be the case is in fact not really the case. According to Davis, the general definition of an interesting theory can be described in the following formula: 'What seems to be X is in reality non-X, or what is accepted as X is actually non-X' (1971: 313).

Based on this general definition Davis developed an index of the interesting, which provides an account of 12 possible ways in which a theory can challenge an audience's assumptions. These 12 ways are in turn subsumed in two main categories.[1] The first category (characterization of a single phenomenon) includes the following seven sub-categories in which we assume that a phenomenon is constituted in a particular way, but in reality it is not, or vice versa: organization, composition, abstraction, generalization, stabilization, function, and evaluation. For example, in the 'organization' category a theory can be made interesting by pointing out that many assume that a specific phenomenon is *disorganized* while it is in fact organized or vice versa. Davis illustrates the first aspect of this category with help of Tonnies's *Community and Society* in which he challenges the assumption at the time that 'all societies are manifold and indeterminate (i.e., disorganized), can in fact be organized around two main types (Gemeinschaft and Gessellschaft)' (1971: 313). An example of the second aspect of the organization category is how Marx, in his *Capital*, challenged the assumption at the time that 'the economic processes of bourgeois society … to be organized in one way, are in fact not organized in that way (but rather organized in another way)' (Davis, 1971: 313). According to Davis, the former aspect of the organization category is often seen in more emerging fields

---

[1] Here, we only provide a couple of examples as a way to illustrate how each category can be used to generate more interesting and influential theories. For a more comprehensive summary of the 12 categories, see Appendix 2 and Davis (1971: 313–26).

while the latter aspect of the category is more commonly used to rejuvenate older and stagnated fields.

Similarly, the 'abstraction' category can be used to generate an interesting theory by challenging the assumption that a phenomenon is *individually* defined by pointing out that it is in fact *holistically* defined or vice versa. In illustrating the first aspect of this sub-category, Davis refers to Durkheim's *Suicide* in which he questions the assumption that suicide is an individual phenomenon by highlighting that it is 'in fact (more crucially) a process characteristic of society' (1971: 316). Hence, what appears to be a property of the individual is in fact a property of a whole society, of which the individual forms a part. Durkheim achieves this challenge by sociologizing something that appears to be an individual phenomenon. An illustration of the second aspect of the abstraction category is how Freud, in *Thoughts for the Times on War and Death*, challenged the prevalent view that 'war' was a social phenomenon by illustrating that it is in fact (more crucially) a psychological phenomenon. Thus, what seems to be a property of some whole 'is actually the property of the individuals which make up this whole' (Davis, 1971: 317). As we can see Freud challenges the assumption that war is a social phenomenon by psychologizing it.

The second category in Davis's index of the interesting (the relations among multiple phenomena) contains five different instances in which we assume that there is a particular relation between multiple phenomena when there is not, and vice versa: co-relation, co-existence, co-variation, opposition and causation. In the 'co-relation' category a theory is made interesting by showing how something that is assumed to be unrelated actually is related. Davis illustrates this move by referring to how Hollingshead, in *Social Class and Mental Illness*, challenged the assumption that mental health and social class are unrelated when in fact they are correlated. Similarly but the reverse, in *Suicide* Durkheim shows that suicide and psychopathological states like race, heredity and climate are uncorrelated not correlated, as was assumed by most people at the time (Davis, 1971: 322).

The 'causation' category is another way to generate an interesting theory by challenging the assumption that an independent phenomenon (variable) in a casual relation is in fact the dependent phenomenon (variable). Davis shows how Becker in *Outsiders*, points out how the odd behavior of some individuals which will 'cause other people to label them "deviants", is in fact caused by other people labeling them deviants' (1971: 326). An example of the reverse challenge is Weber, who in *Protestant Ethics* challenges the common idea at the time that the religion of a society is 'determined by the economy of the society' (1971: 326) by claiming that it is in fact the religion that determines the economy of society.

During the last four decades, many researchers have confirmed and elaborated on Davis's original thesis in various ways (Astley, 1985; Davis, 1999; Hargens, 2000; Weick, 1989, 2001; Wicker, 1985). For example, McKinley et al. (1999) showed that for a theory to receive attention and establish a new theoretical school, it must differ significantly from, and at the same time be connected to, the established literature in order to be seen as meaningful. Likewise, Bartunek et al.'s study of what the board members of a journal considered to be particularly interesting empirical articles provided 'support for Davis's (1971) arguments regarding theory: empirical articles that challenge current assumptions are also particularly likely to be viewed as interesting' (2006: 12).

Corley and Gioia (2011) came to a similar conclusion in their extensive investigation of what constitutes a significant theoretical contribution in organization studies. They show that the most influential theoretical contributions do not offer incremental insights but what they called 'revelatory insights', that is, theoretical insights that challenge and transform our present understanding a specific subject matter. As they argued: 'Our synthesis of the existing literature thus points to insights based in original, especially revelatory, or even transformative thinking as a key factor affecting the attribution of a theoretical contribution at many eminent journals in organization study' (2011: 18). The importance of challenging assumptions and creating novelty is further supported by Hargens's (2000) study about how researchers use references. He shows, hardly surprisingly, that studies that have broken new ground are significantly more cited than those that primarily build on foundational articles in an already established research area.

However, as both Davis (1971, 1986) and Bartunek et al. (2006) noted, a study will not be seen as interesting if it denies all of the audience's assumptions. If the audience's whole assumption ground is disputed, it is likely that most readers will regard the study as irrelevant and absurd. Instead, it is those studies that challenge some, but not all, of the readers' assumptions that will be regarded as interesting and important. Similarly, in their study of what is necessary for a theory to become established as a new theoretical school, McKinley et al. (1999) emphasize the importance of a balance between novelty and continuity. In order to receive attention, a theory must differ significantly from the existing ones at the same time as it must be connected to established literature in order to be seen as meaningful.

Does gap-spotting lead to interesting theories?

According to Davis and the extensive body focusing on 'interestingness' in theory development, what makes a theory interesting and influential is that it deliberately challenges some of an audience's assumptions about an aspect of reality in a significant way. However, if we look at how the researchers describe their construction of research questions in the 119 journal articles analyzed in Chapter 3, none of them actually make an ambitious, deliberate attempt to challenge the assumptions underlying existing theories about the subject matter in question.

It is, however, important to note that gap-spotting rarely involves a simple identification of obvious gaps in a given body of literature. Instead, it consists of complex, constructive and sometimes creative processes. As the findings above illustrate and, in particular, Locke and Golden-Biddle's (1997) study shows, researchers commonly construct gaps by arranging existing studies in specific ways. A gap in the existing literature may also be defined by specific negotiations between researchers, editors and reviewers about which studies actually constitute the existing literature and what is lacking from that domain of literature (Bedeian, 2003, 2004; Tsang and Frey, 2007). Moreover, gap-spotting is not something fixed: it may differ in both scope and complexity, ranging from identifying or constructing fairly narrow gaps to more significant gaps that can lead to important revisions and development of the literature (Colquitt and Zapata-Phelan, 2007).

Furthermore, as described above gap-spotting strategies also sometimes include various questioning moves, such as critical confrontation and the claiming of a new idea. Nevertheless, regardless of variations in scope and complexity, and regardless of the fact that researchers often creatively construct gaps in the existing literature and criticize it for being deficient in some way (for example, for being incomplete, inadequate, inconclusive or underdeveloped), they rarely *challenge* the literature's underlying assumptions in any significant way. Instead, they *build* on (or around) the existing literature to formulate research questions. In other words, whether researchers merely identify or creatively construct gaps in existing literature, they still adhere to the same purpose – namely, 'gap-filling' – that is, adding something to existing literature, *not* identifying and challenging its underlying assumptions, and, based on that, formulating new and original research questions.

Gap-spotting's prevalence in both quantitative and qualitative research

The dominance of gap-spotting is not, as one may assume, confined to quantitative or qualitative hypothetico-deductive research, it is also prevalent within qualitative-inductive research. This is clearly the case in the findings reported above, consisting of a mix of qualitative and quantitative studies, but particularly noticeable in Locke and Golden-Biddle's (1997) investigation of 82 qualitative studies, of which a large majority had an inductive research design. The prevalence of gap-spotting in qualitative inductive research is also evident in Lee et al.'s (1999) review of qualitative research in organizational science during the period 1979–1999, as well in Bluhm et al.'s (2010) follow-up study of the period 1999–2008. Colquitt and Zapata-Phelan's (2007) study of trends in the theoretical contribution and impact of theory-building research and theory-testing research based on a sample of 770 articles published in the *Academy of Management Journal* between 1963 and 2007, further substantiates the dominance of gap-spotting. Their results indicated 'that the typical [inductive research] article published in *AMJ* during our five decade span either examined effects that had been the subject of prior theorizing or introduced a new mediator or moderator of an existing relationship or process' (2007: 1290).

The widespread activity of gap-spotting in qualitative inductive research is further confirmed in recent editorial advice in the *Academy of Management Journal* to researchers and reviewers about what characterizes high-quality qualitative research. According to the editor, an important feature of high-quality qualitative inductive research is that it discusses 'why this qualitative research is needed … For inductive studies, articulating one's motivation not only involves reviewing the literature to illustrate some "gaps" in prior research, but also explaining why it is important to fill this gap. The latter is often forgotten' (Pratt, 2009: 858).

Gap-spotting spans paradigmatic camps

The prevalence of gap-spotting is not only apparent in hypothetico-deductive and qualitative-inductive research, i.e. traditional empirical research, but also spans theoretical camps, from positivists to critical theorists and poststructuralists. For example, Case and Phillipson (2004) (who work within a poststructuralist framework informed by Foucault and Burrell's work) describe their ways of constructing research questions as gap-spotting by identifying an under-researched area: 'To the best of our knowledge, there have been no reputable investigations of the influence of astrology and alchemy on practices within the contemporary worlds of organization and management' (2004: 473). Similarly, Vaara et al., (2005) (who apply a linguistic-power framework informed by power theorists, such as Clegg and Foucault, together with post-colonial research) justify their research question by spotting natural languages as an overlooked area in organization studies: 'Organizational scholars have examined language use in organizational processes and practices and highlighted the culture-knowledge-power linkages from the early 1970s ... [n]atural languages have, however, received very little explicit attention by organization scholars' (2005: 597).

The same applies to almost all the studies discussed by Locke and Golden-Biddle (1997). Only 8 out of 82 used an incommensurability strategy, and did so only to a limited extent. When researchers adopt a critical perspective, it often involves certain challenges, and the outcomes may be quite upsetting for people who hold conventional beliefs. Yet when it comes to formulating research questions, those researchers often accept the existence of a particular subject matter, such as Watson (2004) did in his study regarding HRM, with the existence of HRM as a subject matter motivating a critical theorist perspective. (Many may find it self-evident that there is something called HRM – whether it is seen as an institution, function, occupation, a discourse, etc. – but this may be misleading or at least be seen as uncritically taken for granted and various assumptions of the 'fact' of HRM can be targeted for problematization. Also the 'discourse' of HRM may be problematized in the sense that a lot of talk framed by a particular label does not mean that it is a 'discourse' – an alternative representation could be a 'babble', expressed under the loose umbrella of a specific label.)

Again: do texts conceal how researchers produce research questions?

The above findings and additional studies showing the prevalence of gap-spotting research in social science studies can, of course, be interpreted in various ways. We argued earlier about the research question actually expressed in the text being the significant one and in many cases the only one that it is really possible to investigate systematically. This is especially the case where there is no clear initial research question or where there are gradually or abruptly changing research objectives that perhaps last for several years. But if one accepts this emphasis on the published research question one should then consider if something interesting goes on 'behind' the research question appearing in the publication.

Rhetorical conventions may influence how authors present their research in published texts. Perhaps some researchers problematize the assumptions that underlie existing theory to generate research questions but use a gap-spotting rhetoric when presenting their research in order to get published (Starbuck, 2003, 2006). Perhaps researchers are far more calculative than they appear to be in research texts. They may be wolves in sheep's clothing in the sense of using gap-spotting as a rhetorical clothing to increase their chances of getting their research published, when in reality, they construct their research questions through the problematization of existing literature.[2] Tsoukas (pers. comm.), for example, pointed out that he and Chia (2002) 'challenged assumptions of stability that have long underlain understandings of organizational change, yet they used gap-spotting language insofar as they say that they aim to build on, extend, and further radicalize current processual understandings of change'. As noted by Starbuck, '[a]uthors can increase their acceptance of their innovations by portraying them as being incremental enhancements of wide-spread beliefs' (2003: 349) (see also Bourdieu, 1996; Knorr-Cetina, 1981; Latour and Woolgar, 1979; Mulkay and Gilbert, 1983, for the difference between researchers' work and their publications).

A closely related explanation of the widespread use of gap-spotting is the political context in which research takes place (Bourdieu, 2004; McMullen and Shepard, 2006). It is well known that tenure, promotion and funding decisions are heavily dependent on publishing regularly in quality journals. Challenging assumptions that underlie existing studies is often risky, since it means questioning existing power relations in a scientific field, which may result in upsetting colleagues, reviewers and editors and, thus, may reduce the chances of having an article published (Bourdieu, 2004; Breslau, 1997; Starbuck, 2003). Therefore, in order to increase the chances of being published, many researchers may carry out gap-spotting rather than more consensus-challenging research.

However, given the increased acknowledgment that challenging the assumptions underlying the existing literature is what makes a theory interesting, it seems odd for authors in general to deliberately choose to construct research questions through gap-spotting. And it seems equally strange if they try to downplay or conceal a strong contribution by dressing it up in gap-spotting rhetoric. Certainly some researchers are being risk averse, perhaps in 'publish or perish' employment situations where writing papers that will get published is an absolute priority and doing something potentially (very) interesting is a secondary concern. For such researchers generating interesting theories is perhaps something that is considered after becoming secure in post. The problem here of course is that the time for generating more challenging contributions may never arrive, if one starts one's career by

---

[2] Given that we consider gap-spotting to be, in many cases, less good as an ideal, we should perhaps vary the expression and ask whether the gap-spotters really are sheep in wolves' clothing?

developing a gap-spotting mode of doing research. But for most people, if they have a challenging idea or the capacity to develop one, it would be reasonable to do something bolder and perhaps more rewarding than gap-spotting. This is particularly the case for very competent researchers and/or those in a safe employment situation. However, it is likely to appeal to others as well, when they have an interesting idea, to go beyond generating incremental contributions. It is also likely that most reviewers would pick up and challenge a discrepancy between a research purpose that was presented in gap-spotting discourse but produced results that challenged the literature.

Moreover, as stated in Chapter 3, irrespective of how researchers actually go about formulating and reformulating their research questions, and regardless of what social and political norms influence their presentation in journal articles, it is in the crafting of the research text that the final research question is constructed: the one that specifies the actual contribution of the study. In other words, assumption-challenging research is of limited value if it is not clearly shown in the published research text. To have an interesting (challenging) idea is almost pointless if it is not presented or read as offering something new and different. There are therefore compelling reasons to take the research questions as stated in the published research text very seriously and not to regard them as less important than the research questions in operation during the early stages of the research project or any possible 'real' research question diplomatically hidden and almost undetectable from the published text.

Conclusion

In this chapter we critically evaluated the extent to which generating research questions through gap-spotting is likely to lead to the development of ideas and theories that are seen as interesting and make an impact. We also considered ways of constructing research questions that may lead to interesting and significant theories. Arguably, gap-spotting questions are not likely to lead to the development of interesting theories because they tend to reproduce rather than challenge the assumptions that underlie existing theories and studies. We point to problematization as an obvious alternative, but conclude that it is rarely used, or at least not in any explicit way. This is surprising given the growing recognition that challenging assumptions is what makes a theory interesting and influential. What is more surprising, though, is that even advocates of the various problematization turns (for example, interpretive, political, linguistic, various constructivists turns, paradigm wars, reflexive methodologies and postmodernism), which actively encourage researchers to challenge assumptions and rethink received wisdom, seem to apply gap-spotting as their preferred way of constructing research questions. There are of course exceptions, and many studies include minor elements of 'problematizations', although they do not typically challenge assumptions in any ambitious sense.

Even though gap-spotting research is unlikely to develop theoretically interesting results this does not mean that gap-spotting research is unimportant. It plays a crucial role in developing existing knowledge through systematic and incremental addition, as well as through identifying and addressing more significant gaps. However, because gap-spotting does not deliberately try to challenge the assumptions that underlie the existing literature, it is less likely to raise the proportion of high-impact theories. We can see an imbalance in many social science fields and an acute lack of ambitious problematization. It therefore seems vital to support and strengthen attempts at more deliberate, systematic and ambitious problematization, both as a research ideal and as a methodology for constructing research questions and, thus, encourage a more 'problematizing science'. This does not necessarily require paradigm-changing efforts, as these are very ambitious and demanding and unrealistic for most researchers. One can also imagine more focused and, in scope, moderate problematizations. What we hope to encourage is something in between the gap-spotter and the paradigm-builder. In order to support this, we develop problematization as a methodology for challenging the assumptions underlying existing literature and, based on that, to formulate research questions that may lead to more interesting and influential theories in the next chapter.

5

PROBLEMATIZATION AS A METHODOLOGY FOR GENERATING RESEARCH QUESTIONS

In the previous two chapters, we first investigated the strategies that researchers use for constructing and formulating research questions from the existing literature. The most prevalent strategy by far is gap-spotting. It is by looking for 'gaps' – either a lack of studies or a shortage in the delivery of conclusive results in existing literature – that research questions are constructed. We thereafter emphasized that gap-spotting research is unlikely to produce interesting and influential knowledge contributions. Gap-spotting studies reinforce rather than challenge existing theories in any significant way – and are therefore incapable of producing something with a high impact.

In order to support efforts to more deliberately and systematically identify and challenge the assumptions underlying the existing literature, we develop in this chapter problematization as a methodology for generating research questions. In the first part of the chapter, we describe the aim and focal point of the methodology, followed by an elaboration of an assumption typology, which specifies which assumptions are open for problematization. In the second part of the chapter, we develop a set of principles for identifying, articulating, and challenging the assumptions underlying existing literature and, based on that, constructing research questions that will lead to the development of new ideas and more interesting and influential theories.

The aim of the problematization methodology

Although gap-spotting and problematization are two distinct ways of constructing research questions from existing studies and theory in a field, it must be recognized that they are not mutually exclusive (Dewey, 1938; Foucault, 1972; Freire, 1970; Locke and Golden-Biddle, 1997; Mills, 1959). Any problematization of a literature domain calls for some scrutiny of particular debates, critiques and possibly previous challenges of the assumptions in the domain. Most gap-spotting efforts also involve some form of modest problematization (in the wider sense of the word – that is, critical scrutiny). However, we do not see gap-spotting as a genuine form of problematization since it does not deliberately try to identify and challenge the assumptions underlying the existing literature in the process of constructing research questions. Still, similar to gap-spotting research, problematization studies also need to review specific domains of the existing literature to see if there have been earlier attempts to problematize an area and make sure they do not just repeat the challenging of existing assumptions and develop new ones that are already present in the literature. Perhaps some would see such a literature review as a form of gap-spotting. But we use the term gap-spotting here to refer to the process of formulating research questions by building positively on earlier work and aiming for knowledge accumulation. Reviewing literatures and relating to existing bodies of work do *not* in themselves qualify as gap-spotting. In this sense not all research includes gap-spotting.

There are stronger elements of problematization in debates between advocates of various schools and paradigms (Abbott, 2001, 2004; Burrell and Morgan, 1979), as well as within more radical orientations, such as postmodernism and critical theory. However, although many of the paradigm warriors and proponents of more radical orientations forcefully critique existing theories, their problematizations are often secondary in the sense that they are more or less 'ready-made' by master thinkers, such as a Baudrillardian (Grandy and Mills, 2004) or a Foucauldian perspective on a particular field (Henriques et al., 1984; Knights and Morgan, 1991; Sauder and Espeland, 2009). Similarly, counter texts, such as Donaldson's (1985), typically aim to defend or reinforce a preferred position but do not offer new points of departure. As Abbott notes, a perspective with a ready-made stance toward social life often has 'stock questions and puzzles about it (as in the feminist's questions "what about *women* and social networks?" "what about a *gendered* concept of narrative?" and so on)' (2004: 85).

We therefore do *not* see such prepackaged or programmatic problematization attempts as genuine either, because *they apply rather than challenge the literature they follow*, thus mainly reproducing the assumptions underlying their own perspective. Instead, our idea is to use problematization as a methodology for challenging the assumptions that underlie not only others' but also one's *own* theoretical position and, based on that, to construct novel research questions. Applying a theoretical framework is clearly different from problematizing it, although there are middle versions, for example, when a framework is (moderately) revised in light of critique. The problematization can also be shaped by a research project that is driven by theory or by subject matter that is approached without a clear theoretical framework. In the former, the researcher needs to be careful about what is brought in and how it may govern the problematization effort. In the latter, the researcher may need to pay more attention to what goes on in the literature within the targeted domain. Hence, when generating research questions it is important to distinguish between programmatic and genuine problematization. Here, we advocate a genuine problematization approach (that is, challenging not only the assumptions that underlie others' but also one's own theoretical position).

Advocating a genuine problematization approach does not mean that a problematizer is 'blank' or position free. A developed pre-understanding is a key feature of any researcher (as an academic and social being), which influences any intellectual enterprise. Any problematization necessarily takes its point of departure within a specific meta-theoretical position (that is, an epistemological and ontological stance [Tsoukas and Knudsen, 2004: ch. 1]) as well as within the cultural framework in which the researcher has been socialized through upbringing, education and work. The ambition is therefore normally not, and nor is it typically possible, to totally undo one's own position; rather, it is to unpack it sufficiently so that some of one's ordinary held assumptions can be scrutinized and reconsidered in the process of constructing novel research questions. This unpacking is crucial because, as Slife and Williams note:

> to truly evaluate and understand the ideas behind other ideas, we must have a point of comparison. We must have some contrast with implicit ideas or they will not look like ideas. They will look like common sense or truth or axioms rather than the points of view that they really are. (1995: 71)

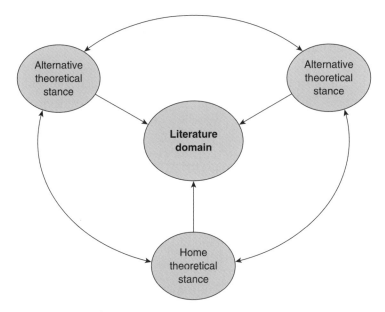

Figure 5.1 *Generating research questions through a dialectical interrogation between the home theoretical stance, alternative stances (1, 2, n stances) and the literature domain*

Hence, as illustrated in Figure 5.1, instead of spotting gaps within a literature domain or applying a prepackaged problematization to challenge the assumptions of others; the aim of the problematization methodology proposed here is to come up with novel research questions through a dialectical interrogation of one's own familiar (or home) position, other theoretical stances, and the domain of literature targeted for assumption challenging. There are of course differences in terms of what a targeted theory domain looks like. Sometimes it is fairly weak, open or pluralistic regarding specific theoretical ideas. Sometimes it is more distinct and may deviate more or less from other ingredients in the interrogation. In some cases it may be difficult to separate between the domain and the home position, in particular if one is an experienced researcher continuing in an area.

In other cases, such as when the home theoretical position and a new domain literature are different, it is easier to separate one's home position from the domain targeted.

The idea of dialectical interrogation calls for the availability of different positions and lines of thinking. This should optimally include some clear variation or difference between the theoretical positions represented by home position, other stances and targeted domain. Such variations in positions provide better opportunities to open up not only the domain literature about the subject matter, but also one's own favored home position. Hence, dialectal interrogation requires the researcher to adopt a counter-stance to their preferred understandings of the world and programmed problematizations and as this is difficult, intellectual resources need to be used. A set up for dialectical interrogation, with position and counter-position initiating dialogue, will offer support. It will stimulate a rethink of one's established ideas and facilitate imagination and a creative reframing of how one conceptualizes and reasons around the subject matter and/or uses a theoretical framework.

Ideas similar to dialectical interrogation have also been suggested in the field of education by Hostetler (1994) through his notion critical dialogue, and in the field of psychology by Yanchar et al. (2008) as part of their 'component in critical thinking practice', as well as by Alvesson and Sköldberg (2009) in suggesting 'reflexive methodology'. In these enterprises, paradigm and other broader debates, such as behaviorism and culturalism; contextualism and non-contextualism; and choice and constraint (Abbott, 2004: 162–210); and critical frameworks, such as political (Foucault, 1977), constructionist (Gergen, 1992), and postmodernist (Rosenau, 1992); as well as counter-responses to these; are seen as important methodological *resources* to open up and scrutinize assumptions underlying established theories, including, to some extent, the favorite theory of the problematizer. Such a problematization methodology also supports a more reflective and inventive scholarly attitude in the sense that it encourages the researcher not only to use his or her own favorite theoretical position but also to start 'using different standard stances to question one another ... [and combining them] into far more complex forms of questioning than any one of them can produce alone' (Abbott, 2004: 87).

Thus, by elaborating and proposing problematization as a methodology for generating research questions, we do not take any particular paradigmatic stance. We do however embrace the general and long-held meta-theoretical assumption within academia that all knowledge is uncertain, truths or theories cannot be accepted as given, researchers tend to be conformist and paradigm bound (Kuhn, 1970) and theoretical developments are partly based on rethinking and challenging the fundamental assumptions underlying dominating theories (Tsoukas and Knudsen, 2004). In other words, problematization, as we define it here, can, in principle, be applied to all theoretical traditions or methodological convictions and can be used within, and against, all, including the problematizer him/herself.

A note on theory

Before elaborating problematization as a methodology for generating research questions more specifically, it is important to describe what we mean by 'theory'. Since there are many views on theories in the social sciences (Colquitt and Zapata-Phelan, 2007; DiMaggio, 1995; Sutton and Staw, 1995), and since these views are in various ways part of what can and should be targeting for assumption challenging, we are not asserting a strict view on theory. Bacharach's (1989) definition probably comes closest to the wide-ranging view of theory that we adopt here. He defines theory as:

> a statement of relations among concepts within a boundary set of assumptions and constraints. It is no more than a linguistic device used to organize a complex empirical world ... the purpose of a theoretical statement is twofold: to organize (parsimoniously) and to communicate (clearly). (1989: 496)

What is particularly close to our own view is his notion that theories are not free-floating statements but are always based on and bounded by researchers' assumptions about the subject matter in question. As Bacharach notes, it is critical to grasp the boundary set of assumptions, because 'if a theory is to be properly used or tested, the theorist's implicit assumptions which form the boundaries of the theory must be understood' (1989: 498). However, understanding the assumptions that underpin existing theories is important, not only to be able to use and test them, but also to be able to develop new theories. In particular, without understanding the assumptions that underlie existing theories, it is not possible to problematize them and, based on that, to construct research questions that may lead to the development of more interesting and influential theories (Davis, 1971).

Challenging assumptions: the focal point in generating research questions through problematization

But how can we problematize assumptions in a way that generates novel research questions? To answer that question we first need to provide a more explicit definition of what we mean by 'problematization' in this study. Problematization is featured in various theoretical orientations, such as pragmatism (Dewey, 1916), actor–network theory (ANT) (Callon, 1980), and in Foucault's extensive work (Foucault, 1984, 1985). Although problematization forms a critical step in Dewey's inquiry approach, it is not particular helpful here, as he does not really elaborate the concept in any specific way but instead devotes most of his attention to how to find solutions to stated problems. As Koopman noted, Dewey 'devoted hundred of pages to the genesis of solution [but] ... hardly ever wrote about the genesis of problem' (2011: 25). In a similar vein, while problematization makes up one of the four key dimensions in the sociology of translation within the ANT camp, it does not seem to provide particular guidelines for how to generate research questions through problematizing the assumptions underlying existing literature.

We regard Foucault's notion of problematization to be a more promising starting point for developing a problematization methodology for generating research questions (Castels, 1994; Deacon, 2000). According to Foucault, problematization is first and foremost an 'endeavour to know how and to what extent it might be possible to think differently, instead of legitimizing what is already known' (1985: 9). Such an endeavor does not primarily question how well some constructs or relationships between constructs represent a particular subject matter like 'motivation' or 'diversity'. Instead, it questions the necessary presuppositions researchers make about a subject matter in order to develop the specific theory about it. As Foucault put it, 'the development of a given into a question ... is what constitutes *the point* of problematization, and the specific work of thought' (Foucault, 1984: 389, emphasis added).

Looking more specifically, in order to think problematically about the subject matter as such we need to move away, at least initially, from what Foucault described as the dialectics of question and answer underlying most research (Castels, 1994, in Flynn, 1994: 42). As became apparent in our review in Chapter 3 of how researchers construct their research questions in relation to the existing literature, questions and answers often go together in a self-confirming and closed circle, as answers to some extent are predetermined by the questions. These often come logically from what others have done and – in particular – not done or have not been able to reach a consensus on. But such questions typically become predictable and unimaginative.

Problematization urges us that instead of trying to formulate and refine a specific research question by reviewing the literature about a given subject matter we need to ask ourselves questions such as the following: How has a certain subject matter become an object of scientific investigation? How have our research questions been produced, and what makes us ask the questions we ask? For instance, what historical and practical conditions have given birth to the subject matter and how have those conditions given birth to it? In particular, we need to ask what determines our current understanding of the subject matter from which we are able to formulate our research questions. Furthermore, we also need, as Bernauer (1987) argued, to ask how the path to our current understanding of the subject matter has been determined, and how exclusions have operated in delineating the subject matter in question.

More specifically, following the lead of Foucault, problematization consists of two interrelated steps. First, the opening up of subject matter for critical inquiry by scrutinizing the ways they have emerged historically and on what assumptions and conditions they rest. Second, the opening up of subject matter in this way enables us to question their underlying assumptions and, based on that, generate new areas of inquiries, potentially leading to new ways of being, doing and thinking.

As a range of scholars have noted (Bourdieu, 1996; Derrida, 1978; Heidegger, 1981; Husserl, 1970; Merleau-Ponty, 1962), assumptions work as a starting point for knowledge production since they always involve some suppositions or, as Gadamer (1994) put it, prejudices about the subject matter in question. As Koch argued 'we cannot discriminate a so-called variable ... without making strong presumptions of philosophical cast about the nature of our human subject matter' (1981: 267). For instance, leadership studies presuppose a set of assumptions that enable us to conceptualize 'leadership' as something in the first place, such as trait theory, emphasizing person-bound, stable qualities. Without such an initial understanding of leadership, we would have no idea what to look for, how to design our study, what empirical material to collect, and how to analyze and theorize leadership. But how can we, as Feyerabend asked:

> possibly examine something we are using all the time? How can we analyze the terms in which we habitually express our most simple and straightforward observations, and reveal their presuppositions? How can we discover the kind of world we presuppose when proceeding as we do? The answer is clear: we cannot discover it from the *inside*. We need an *external* standard of criticism, we need a set of alternative assumptions. (1978: 31)

This is what the problematization methodology enables us to do. The focal point in problematization as a methodology for generating research questions is *to illuminate and challenge those assumptions underlying existing theories (including one's own favorite theories) about a specific subject matter.*

In order to develop problematization as a methodology for generating research questions, two key questions need to be answered regarding assumptions. First, what *types* of assumptions are relevant? Second, *how* can these assumptions be identified, articulated and challenged in a way that is likely to lead to the development of an interesting theory? Of relevance here is the growing body of work that has focused on 'interestingness' in theory development. As pointed out in Chapter 4, Davis (1971) has discussed what makes a theory interesting and influential most fully through his 'index of the interesting', consisting of 12 different ways in which an audience's assumptions can be challenged (see also Appendix 2).

While Davis's index provides a comprehensive account of the ways in which a theory can challenge an audience's assumptions, the index does not specify what types of assumptions can be problematized. It provides only a general definition of assumption in the form of 'what seems to be X is in reality non-X, or what is accepted as X is actually non-X' (Davis, 1971: 313). In particular, such a general definition does not address how assumptions differ in character (Brookfield, 1995), depth (Abbott, 2004; Schein, 1985) and scope (Gouldner, 1970), which is essential to know when constructing research questions through problematization. Nor does the index provide any specific principles for how different types of assumptions can be identified, articulated and challenged. Below we develop a typology of assumptions that specifies what types of assumptions are available for problematization when generating research questions, followed by an elaboration of a set of principles for how assumptions can be identified and challenged.

A typology of assumptions open to problematization

While there is a range of different assumptions within the scientific field, we find it productive to distinguish five broad sets of assumptions that differ in both depth and scope. These are in-house, root metaphor, paradigm, ideology and field assumptions. This categorization is partly inspired by Morgan's (1980) differentiation between puzzle solving, root metaphors and paradigms. The typology is also influenced by the paradigm debate in which some authors claim to have an overview of various world views (paradigms), thereby indicating the significance of the wider arena held together by some overall ideas and assumptions (Burrell and Morgan, 1979). An interest in ideology assumptions proceeds from the observation that researchers' engagement in scientific fields is in no way neutral regarding human interests and political positioning (Habermas, 1972). The notion of field assumption is inspired by scholars who take a broader view of an academic area (e.g., Bourdieu, 1979; Foucault, 1972).

In-house assumptions exist within a particular school of thought in the sense that they are shared and accepted as unproblematic by its advocates. In-house assumptions differ from puzzle solving in that they refer to a set of ideas held by a theoretical school about a specific subject matter, whereas puzzle solving refers to the particular way of conducting research stipulated by that school. An example of in-house assumptions is trait theories within the rationalistic school, which typically conceptualize leadership as a set of specific attributes, such as the formal knowledge, skills, attitudes and personal traits possessed by an individual leader (Yukl, 2006). If we were to question that leadership is defined less by the technical knowledge leaders possess than by their verbal skills, we would challenge an in-house assumption of leadership research. In other words, by challenging the importance of technical knowledge for explaining leadership we only challenge the importance of an existing trait, not the trait theory as such. That is why it is a challenge of an in-house assumption.

Root metaphor assumptions are associated with broader images of a particular subject matter (Atkinson and Checkland, 1984; Morgan, 1980, 1997). Within organization studies, for example, it is common to see organizations as 'cultures' in terms of a unitary set of values and beliefs shared by organization members. However, at the root metaphor level (Smircich, 1983), authors have questioned assumptions around unity, uniqueness and consensus, and they have emphasized differentiation, fragmentation, discontinuity and ambiguity as key elements in culture (Martin, 2002; Martin and Meyerson, 1988). Within higher education studies, the university institution is viewed as a sieve, incubator, temple and a hub (Stevens et al., 2008), as well as a site for keeping young people occupied and unemployment down, and as an amplifier of status claims for groups wanting to become professionals (Alvesson, 2013a).

The ontological, epistemological and methodological assumptions that underlie a specific literature can be characterized as *paradigmatic assumptions* (Brookfield, 1995; Burrell and Morgan, 1979; Husen, 1988; Kuhn, 1970; Ritzer, 1980). The challenge of such assumptions is often a central element in generating interesting research questions. For example, by adopting an interpretive perspective on professional competence, Sandberg (2000) challenged the dualist ontology underlying the prevalent rationalistic school, which conceptualizes professional competence as consisting of two separate entities: a set of attributes possessed by the worker and a separate set of work activities. However, from an interpretive approach, competence does not consist of two separate entities; instead, person and work form an inseparable relation through the lived experience of work. Such a questioning enabled Sandberg to provide an alternative assumption ground and, based on that, to generate new research questions about professional competence.

Ideology assumptions include various political-, moral- and gender-related assumptions held about the subject matter. Burawoy (1979), for example, suggested that researchers conducting studies of work should not proceed from the question 'Why don't workers work harder?' and then investigate norms about a reasonable work performance; instead, they should ask, 'Why do people work as hard as they do?' In a similar vein, Sievers (1986) challenged existing theories of motivation by suggesting that instead of asking how people can be motivated in organizations, they should ask why people need to be motivated at all if they experience their jobs as meaningful. Likewise, in marketing Peter and Olson (1986: 111) challenged the common idea that marketing is a science by urging us to turn the tables and ask, 'Is science marketing?' A common ideology assumption in education is 'that good adult educational processes are inherently democratic' (Brookfield, 1995: 3).

Field assumptions are a broader set of assumptions about a specific subject matter that are shared by several different schools of thought within a paradigm, and sometimes even across paradigms and disciplines. Simon's (1947) work on bounded rationality can perhaps be seen as a mild but successful identification and challenge of a field assumption. His challenge of the widely shared assumption that humans are rational decision makers, and the alternative assumption of bounded rationality, opened up a range of new and interesting research questions and theories. Field assumptions may also unite antagonistic schools, which, at one level, often present as different and even oppositional but, at a deeper level, share a set of assumptions about their particular field (cf. Bourdieu, 1979). For example, labor process theorists and poststructural-oriented critical management scholars agree that there is something called 'management' and an ideology or discourse of managerialism, which should be critically addressed. However, in debates each of these schools of thought claims to have privileged access to an insightful understanding of management.

Taken together, the typology can be seen as a continuum of overlapping assumptions open for problematization, where in-house assumptions form one end and field assumptions the other end of the continuum. Challenging in-house assumptions can be seen as a minor form of problematization; questioning root metaphor assumptions as a more middle-range form; and challenging paradigm, ideology and field assumptions as a broader and more fundamental form of problematization. It may seem that challenging any of the three latter types of assumptions is most likely to generate research questions that may lead to the development of more interesting and influential theories. However, a challenge of these broader assumptions may also be superficial, since it is difficult to achieve depth and precision when addressing broad intellectual terrains. An insightful challenge of an in-house or a root metaphor assumption can be a key part in the process of developing new theory. More important than the range of assumptions challenged and the development of something novel is the quality of the problematization and the surprise factor it generates. The surprise factor is likely to be higher if one problematizes an assumption that has been unchallenged and taken for granted for many years.

We should add that it is often difficult to establish the exact range of an assumption, that is, to firmly place it as an in-house, metaphor and so on assumption. For example, attempts to identify a paradigm and its boundaries often differ. Kuhn (1970) himself was notoriously imprecise and incoherent in his view of paradigm. Efforts to specify Kuhn's notion of paradigm in sociology have resulted in several different versions, ranging from two to eight paradigms (Eckberg and Hill, 1980). As these authors remark, 'the sociological pie can be sliced in many ways' (p. 123). One can therefore not expect precise and authoritative establishments of assumption levels.

The purpose of the overview of assumptions is not necessarily to encourage efforts to establish the level or range of assumptions. Rather, our intention is to point out that there is a spectrum of assumptions: from being shared only by advocates of a specific theory or a school to assumptions virtually shared by everyone belonging to a research field and possibly even including different paradigms. Having a good feeling for levels and types is thus important in order to work with assumptions in a qualified way but does not necessarily involve precision in locating these in terms of an exact range or levels. In many cases the researcher may feel it best to refrain from exact statements in this respect.

Methodological principles for identifying, articulating and challenging assumptions

As described above, a key task in generating research questions through problematization is to enter a dialectical interrogation between one's own and other meta-theoretical stances so as to identify, articulate and challenge the central assumptions underlying the existing literature in a way that opens up new areas of inquiry. To be able to problematize assumptions through such an interrogation, the following methodological principles are central: (1) identifying a domain of literature; (2) identifying and articulating the assumptions underlying this domain; (3) evaluating these; (4) developing an alternative assumption ground; (5) considering it in relation to its audience; and (6) evaluating the alternative assumption ground.

While we, for the sake of clarity, present the principles in a sequential order, the actual problematization process is considerably more iterative than linear in character. There is likely to be a strong tendency to move sequentially from (1) to (6) but there are often other possible moves. During a later stage one may for example feel inspired or forced to revise the identification of the domain. Alternatively, an evaluation of an alternative assumption ground and the research question that follows may lead to more work with identifying existing assumptions and/or formulating new ones. Moreover, these principles should not be treated as a list of fixed ingredients in a recipe but, rather, as important elements to consider in the problematization process. Some of these may be sidestepped or combined.

Sometimes a researcher may more or less spontaneously produce counter-assumptions in a creative way without much careful, systematic and critical analysis preceding and supporting the efforts to creatively develop something novel. As Deacon (2000) notes, problematization cannot be reduced to a mechanical or even strictly analytical procedure, since it always involves some kind of creative act: 'It is a creation in the sense that, given a certain situation, one cannot infer that precisely this kind of problematization will follow' (2000: 135). The problem of strict and mechanical rule following in knowledge production is also well described by Feyerabend (1978) in his classic book *Against Method*. Recognizing this should, however, not prevent us from realizing that simply relying on creativity is often not so helpful. 'Be creative!' is advice of minimal value. The systematic, diligent work with texts aiming to interpret and/or construct dominant assumptions and examine their possibly problematic or constraining character and then develop, refine, revise and formulate alternative assumptions can to some extent be structured. In other words, creativity can productively be supplemented by the methodology for assumption-scrutinizing and questioning.

1. Identifying a domain of literature for assumption-challenging investigations

It is usually not obvious how to sort and delimit existing studies into a specific domain of literature and then relate that literature to one's own study (Locke and Golden-Biddle, 1997). The boundaries of the existing literature in a field are often difficult to define. Mostly, existing labels like power, knowledge, culture and discourse may not say that much. Using established conventions for structuring fields or relying on popular labels for sorting literatures may also be counterproductive. Literature sorting is therefore often tricky and arbitrary irrespective of whether one is using gap-spotting or problematization as a way of constructing research questions. However, compared to gap-spotting research, problematization efforts are less concerned with covering all possible studies within a field than with uncritically reproducing the assumptions informing these studies. Problematization research typically involves a more narrow literature coverage and in-depth readings of key texts, with the specific aim of identifying and challenging the assumptions underlying the specific literature domain targeted. In this sense, the prevailing norm to relate one's own study to all the relevant literature works against problematization and needs to be resisted. However, it is important to make broad references to major or typical studies and to scrutinize possible problematization attempts in relevant work.

It is important to consider two interrelated issues when identifying a domain of literature for problematization: the actual domain targeted and the specific texts chosen for deep readings and re-readings. Identifying or constructing a domain of literature provides the entrance to picking some texts, but a careful reading of these may inspire the revision of the literature domain that finally will be the target for the research question. One possibility is to focus on an exemplar – that is, a path-defining study (Abbott, 2001; Kuhn, 1970) – that plays a key role in a literature domain.

Given the significance of path-defining studies, such a focus may be productive, although, of course, later work drawing on the path-defining study needs to be identified and reviewed in order to investigate whether all the assumptions that one finds potentially interesting to challenge are still in operation. This is often difficult as there are critiques, debates and minor or major revisions of path-defining research that confuse which assumptions are still relevant to problematize (one may also want to examine classical texts as a value in itself and be less concerned with exactly what is guiding contemporary research, but this is a slightly different objective from the one we are addressing here, aiming to produce good and novel research questions). Another option is to concentrate on one summary or a few authoritative summaries, given that they are not too general and wide in scope (which may mean that the clues to assumptions are too vague). A third option is to look at a few more recent, influential, and respected pieces, covering some variation in a particular domain of literature. Although these options need to be supplemented with broader readings, the in-depth reading of the selected texts is the focal point for the problematizer.

2. Identifying and articulating the assumptions underlying the chosen domain of literature

Assumptions underlying a specific domain of literature are rarely explicitly formulated. Sometimes, we do however find clearly stated assumptions, such as 'individuals always try to maximize their self-interest' in economic studies or 'language constitutes reality' in discourse studies. Such explicitly formulated assumptions are more like 'postulations'. But behind postulations and beside explicit assumptions we find assumptions that are implicit and often taken for granted. As Gouldner notes, postulations 'contain a second set of assumptions that are unpostulated and unlabeled. ... because they provide the background out of which the postulations in part emerge and ... not being expressively formulated, they remain in the background of the theorist's attention' (1970: 29). Similarly, Mahrer (2000) shows how the field of psychotherapy rests on a range of well-hidden assumptions or foundational beliefs that guide both researchers and practitioners. As Mahrer points out, foundational beliefs in psychotherapy are often camouflaged in commonly used concepts and 'phrases as *conditioned response, borderline disorder*, or *anal stages of development*, one is likely to have bought, perhaps without fully appreciating, entire sets of underlying foundational beliefs that provide the supporting conceptual meaning and structure for such innocent-appearing terms and phrases' (2000: 1118, original emphasis). It is these kinds of beliefs or assumptions, those that mostly remain implicit or weakly articulated, that are the main target in the problematization methodology. However, it may be worthwhile to also question long-standing explicit assumptions in a particular area. This is particularly the case if they are frequently stated but taken-for-granted and seen as something more or less natural and true.

A key issue here is to transform what are commonly seen as truths or facts into assumptions. In doing so the implicit or hidden is made explicit and laid open to scrutiny. This often calls for a hermeneutic process of noting, interpreting, moving between and reinterpreting different cues, indicating assumptions not directly expressed, nor perhaps being consciously grasped or considered by authors. Hermeneutic ideas such as the circle (constant and recurrent moves) between pre-understanding and understanding are helpful here (Alvesson and Sköldberg, 2009).

Drawing on the assumption typology outlined above, we see a range of methodological tactics available for identifying the assumptions in existing literature. In-house assumptions can be identified by scrutinizing internal debates and the interfaces between a specific group of authors who frequently refer to each other and neighboring areas, moderately relating one's work to the focused group's work, and mainly using a similar narrative style and vocabulary. For example, various authors have challenged the idea that organizations typically form unitary and unique cultures (Van Maanen and Barley, 1984), or even clear and stable subcultures (Martin and Meyerson, 1988), by seeing culture as a process – a form of traffic – rather than as something stable (Alvesson, 2013b).

Root metaphor assumptions can be explored by (1) identifying the basic image or metaphor of social reality informing a text or school and (2) detecting or producing alternative possible confrontational metaphors. Morgan's (1986) *Images of Organization* provides one well-known illustration of how metaphors can be used to become aware of alternative conceptualizations and, thus, how they can inspire one to articulate one's own assumptions. Alvesson (1993) picks up this line, arguing that it is possible to carve out assumptions by looking at the metaphors behind the metaphors used (that is, second-level metaphors). For example, behind the metaphor that conceptualizes organization as a political arena, one could imagine different views of this arena, one being a parliamentary democracy (with the rules of the game) and another being more like a jungle, where the political battles are less civilized and rule bound.

Identifying paradigm assumptions normally calls for some familiarity with an alternative worldview, without being stuck in the latter. Some existing efforts to map and confront paradigms may be helpful (e.g., Burrell and Morgan, 1979; Ritzer, 1980). Although reading about paradigm debates can be useful, the challenge is not to be caught up in them or by the positions expressed in those debates. Instead, they should be used as important heuristic tools to loosen up the views of others as well as our own (Abbott, 2004: 86).

Ideological assumptions can also be explored by being aware of positions that are very different from the focal one in terms of interests, focus, identifications, values and ethical commitments. One tactic would be to read and interpret an example of what appears to be positive and worth taking seriously as a problem to be addressed or as a solution to be embraced. Another tactic would be to view something negative (for example, repressive) as perhaps innocent or even positive (for example, child labor – in moderate doses, under-regulated circumstances – as valuable for families in poor countries and a more positive form of socialization than the consumerist and hedonistic forms of upbringing perhaps dominating in wealthy countries and families). Working with the recognition of a multitude of interests and values, and the contradictions and dilemmas evident between these, could also be beneficial. The contradiction between values like autonomy and leadership or free speech versus political correctness could exemplify this.

Field assumptions are difficult to identify because 'everyone' shares them, and, thus, they are rarely thematized in research texts. One option is to search across theoretical schools and intellectual camps to see whether they have anything in common regarding the conceptualization of the particular subject matter in question. Another option is to look at debates and critiques between seemingly very different positions and focus on what they are *not* addressing – that is, the common consensual ground not being debated. Looking at other fields may also be valuable in gaining some perspective. This is to some extent illustrated in this book, since we identify and challenge gap-spotting as a field assumption for how to generate research questions within our field, organization studies – as well as in other disciplines – in this regard, we acknowledge help from Davis (1971), a scholar outside our field.

Although focusing on a specific type of assumption may be fruitful, it is often better to vary one's focus and, at least initially, consider what in-house, metaphor, paradigm, ideology and field assumptions underlie a particular domain of existing literature. It is also important to focus on assumptions that may exist at different theoretical levels within a targeted study. This is because challenging an in-house assumption related to a broader theoretical perspective (for example, symbolic interactionist perspective) within the targeted study may facilitate the formulation of more interesting research questions than challenging an in-house assumption underlying a specific theory (for example, human capital theory) within the study targeted. It should also be borne in mind that assumptions are not fixed but are, to some extent, an outcome of how one constructs the nature and scope of the domain of literature targeted, and this can be narrowed or broadened and can be interpreted in different ways. Hence, the combination of hermeneutical in-depth readings, creative efforts, some boldness, patience, self-critique, support from theoretical stances other than one's own, and sometimes even luck is important in order to identify and articulate assumptions.

A particularly important ingredient to enable creatively in identifying assumptions is to engage in perspective shifting. This means that a variety of theoretical ideas are invoked in order to open up a sensitivity for various assumptions, as researchers with problematization ambitions – like other mortals – we do not only function intellectually. It is also important to realize our emotional preferences and how our own identity can give rise to blindness, one-sightedness or a general reduced ability to seriously consider other aspects than those we normally tend to see. It is therefore important to try to work with one's own identity and associated emotional commitments and blinders, such as through distancing and identity shifting. For example, distancing and identity shifting can be done by accessing alternative theories, talking to people with views different from one's own and by voluntarily trying to step into the shoes of advocates of other perspectives (associated with various paradigms, knowledge interests, theories, social identities). A critical researcher may try to identify him- or herself with a person in charge of an organization or another elite representative. A symbolic interactionist may try to take the outlook of a macro researcher seriously. A poststructuralist may think about a problem that calls for a solution – rather than a deconstructionist ironic reading – and then imagine him- or herself as a functionalist trying to deliver a robust and clear result. All these moves aim to increase imagination and facilitate the often rather difficult project of identifying assumptions.

Since not all assumptions are likely to be strong candidates for problematization and the development of new assumptions and research questions, it is often good to identify a surplus of assumptions that can be challenged and to formulate these in various ways, offering different possibilities for further work. In later stages of the process some initially interesting assumptions may be reassessed as less interesting to challenge as initially thought. One could also use the tactic of identifying a few assumptions that appear promising for challenging but if none of these can fully be developed into interesting new assumptions, then one could make a second, new effort to develop more potentially interesting assumptions, that is, to go from later stages in the model back to stage 2.

3. Evaluating articulated assumptions

Having identified and articulated assumptions within the chosen literature domain, the problematizer needs to assess them. Certainly not all assumptions are worthy of being problematized and brought forward as significant research contributions – or as key steps in such an enterprise. The problematizer must therefore continually ask him/herself, What is the theoretical potential of challenging a particular assumption? Is this novel? Is it likely to stimulate non-trivial rethinking? In what way may this lead to productive new research questions? As a general rule, challenging broader assumptions, such as paradigm or field assumptions, is likely to lead to greater impact theories, but these assumptions are often more difficult to identify and challenge successfully, and they may also be broad and imprecise. And as mentioned, it is the novelty of a 'that's interesting' insight that is crucial, not the scope of the problematization. But it is of course always better if one can say something that is novel and inspirational for a larger rather than a smaller audience.

An overall but vague consideration for an identified assumption to be problematized should be that it does not contribute significantly to a 'good' understanding of the subject matter but is still broadly shared within a research area. 'Good' here has three aspects, often difficult to separate in practice. One is that the identified assumption is false, misleading, narrow or in another ways leading to a poor understanding of the subject matter. Another is that the identified assumption does not add much of intellectual value, perhaps as a result of it being around for some time and the generative capacity having been lost, leading to only very minor additional research results that are of interest. A third concerns the practical value of an assumption, that is, the relevance and value of knowledge outside an academic context of interestingness (for researchers interested in theory).

The first aspect, 'truth' in any of the several available senses is always an important criterion to consider – that is, an assumption that is seen as 'untrue' is then targeted. Empirical evidence indicating that some assumptions are problematic is important here, and careful consideration of existing empirical studies should always inform the judgment of the problematizer. At the same it is also important to not have too much faith in empirical studies, as they always rely upon assumptions and some of these may be problematic. For example, there is a wealth of questionnaire-based studies of national cultures and their impact on behavior, based on assumptions about homogeneous and static cultures having causal effects. However, the results from these studies can be questioned. Even if they deliver seemingly robust and impressive empirical results these studies may conceal basic problems and be questioned in fundamental ways (McSweeney, 2002). One should also add that assumptions – like paradigms – can seldom be directly empirically investigated or tested, as they are always implicated in, and guide, research (Astley, 1985; Kuhn, 1970).

The second aspect concerns the possibilities of developing new ideas or insights by considering other aspects than those previously focused on. This means playing down the truth (empirical support) criterion. Truth as such is often difficult to determine and is not the same thing as valuable knowledge. Something true can also be trivial or useless, and an insistence on proving that something is true (where a hypothesis should be verified) can be constraining (Becker, 1998: 20–4; Starbuck, 2006: 99–101). Most complex, important and interesting research then escapes simple hypotheses testing. Theoretical fruitfulness, novelty and provocative capacity can be equally, if not more, important to bear in mind – and are typically what makes a theory interesting (Astley, 1985). A theoretical contribution may also be about discovering a new aspect or offering a reframing, leading to a broader or qualitatively different understanding of a subject matter, which often goes far beyond issues of whether knowledge claims are empirically supported or not.

A closely related criterion is to what extent a challenge of the identified assumptions can inspire new areas of research and research programs. The articulated assumptions may also be assessed in terms of how they form the basis for other established knowledge areas or a dominant line of thinking that tends to produce mainstream effects (for example, constrain imagination and close alternatives). 'Timing' is another consideration. An assumption may be productive and inspiring at a specific time but may gradually become part of conventional wisdom and lose its power to generate new knowledge. Many critical perspectives (poststructuralism, critical discourse analysis, feminism) may, for example, be able to inspire problematization for some time but may later establish a new set of unchallenged assumptions – a source of application rather than drivers for rethinking. Problematizing such assumptions may then be necessary, either through informed defenses of the problematized positions (Donaldson, 1985) or through new or synthesized approaches, such as skeptical partial affirmation (Newton, 1998).

The third aspect considers the practical significance of an alternative assumption. The assumption should not just be intellectually interesting for academics, but should also have a clear relevance for important social, economical or political issues. While this is not the primary concern for research aiming to produce interesting new ideas, it should be borne in mind in the evaluation process. The fact that certain theories or ideas are influential is probably related to their being seen by many people as having a bearing on something important. It is also imperative to reduce our narcissistic and egocentric tendencies that prioritize what we find interesting ourselves and what can promote our careers and status in the academic community.

4. Developing an alternative assumption ground

While the formulation of alternative assumptions analytically marks a crucial stage in problematization, it should not be seen as isolated from the other principles involved. The (re)formulation part extends the earlier parts of the process: identifying assumptions calls for at least an intuitive idea of alternative assumptions, and success in the former means that the latter is likely to come through more clearly.

Similar to identifying and articulating existing assumptions, it can be useful to consult available critical and reflexive literature, representatives of competing schools, and various forms of heuristic tools, such as those offered by Abbott (2004),[1] in developing new assumptions. As emphasized above, a challenge of existing assumptions should include some independence from these and should move beyond already available counter-assumptions. It therefore involves more than a literature review of the gap-spotting type, as it calls for a broader overview and a broader set of considerations than vacuum-cleaning a sub-field for an empty space to plug in one's own study. It may, for example, be tempting to use an interpretive stance against functionalist assumptions, to apply critical realist ideas to social constructionist studies, to replace interpretive humanism with poststructuralism or to let process thinking loose on anything that may be seen as an expression of stability or entity assumptions (systems, structures, traits). Nevertheless, the purpose of the approach suggested here is to avoid such moves. To repeat, genuine problematization as defined in this book is not programmatic. Producing new and good research questions means that there are no predefined answers available; new questions offer starting points for new answers. Such a problematization is facilitated by temporarily applying the dialectical interrogation between different theoretical stances and the domain of literature targeted. The idea is to be inspired by various theoretical stances and their resources and to use them creatively in order to come up with something unexpected and novel.

One way of generating an alternative assumption ground is to use what Feyerabend (1978: 29–33) called counter-induction. It means comparing assumptions from different theoretical positions that are inconsistent with each other, in particular with one's own favorite theoretical position. Such inconsistency comparison

---

[1] Appendix 3 provides a summary of Abbott's main heuristic tools.

may produce a set of alternative assumptions that enable us to construct and formulate new research questions.

Another possibility to come up with an alternative assumption ground is to use analogy as an heuristic tool. As Abbott (2004) suggests, one can make an analogy by trying to understand a particular subject matter with the help of a completely different subject matter outside your own field. Abbott points to how Hannan and Freeman's (1977) study created a new school within organization studies by making an analogy with ecology, thus regarding organizations as ecological systems, and with Becker (1998), who opened up a whole new research area by regarding racial discrimination as an economic phenomenon. As Abbott points out, such analogies not only help us to see our topic in a new light, they also enable us to use the whole machinery of models and concepts from the analogical field to further analyze and interpret the subject matter in question.

Making a reversal is another heuristic suggested by Abbott (2004), which could also be productively used for creating an alternative assumption ground. For example, for most people it is self-evident that universities facilitate learning. Making a reversal would then be to claim that universities do not facilitate but prevent learning. Abbott points to a very successful reversal made by DiMaggio and Powell in their well-known (1983) paper 'The iron cage revisited'. In that paper they make a reversal of Hannan and Freeman's (1977) question of why there are so many types of organizations by asking 'why do all organizations look alike?' (2004: 129). Another example would be to claim that terrorism is good rather than bad. Such a claim may be seen as outrageous but it can also open up new avenues for research. For instance, it may highlight that terrorism unites patriotic people gathering against the threat and for the military and the police who get extra funding and the resources they want, all in the name of fighting terrorism. It may also help us to become more aware of a range of assumptions that underlie our understanding of 'terrorism' and, thus, enable us to make more nuanced distinctions between different meanings of terrorism.

Alternative assumptions need to be formulated in a way that points to a new pathway for theoretical exploration or empirical study. This includes a preliminary theoretical (re)conceptualization of the subject matter, which provides a direction to further study but without prescribing a fixed outcome. As described in Chapter 2, a genuine research question is fairly open and should provide a line of thinking but not predetermine the answer. Developing the alternative assumption ground, therefore, involves crafting and fine-tuning the way this is being expressed. In order to accomplish the intended effect of creating surprise, challenging received wisdom and opening up to the unexpected, it is important to consider what has rhetorical appeal. The aesthetic dimensions of the alternative assumption ground are also central in composing an appealing and convincing argument (Astley, 1985). For instance, to achieve the response of 'that's interesting', it is important to work with metaphors and other language resources that are appealing, and with concepts and formulations that make an impression and are memorable.

Examples from our own home discipline, organization studies, could be March and Olsen's (1976) garbage can model of decision making and Brunsson's (2003) idea of organized hypocrisy. The garbage can model rejects the idea of rational decision making and claims that decisions are often made on a random basis – when streams of decision opportunities, people, problems and solutions meet. Sometimes a solution may be circling around, like a skills improvement program at the same time somebody is concerned about local unemployment. If advocates of the solution meet people worried about local unemployment at a time when there is some extra money available, and a key player skeptical of skills improvement programs is not present, a decision is likely to be made. Careful and rational analysis proceeding from the problem and careful consideration of a range of solutions are, according to March and Olsen, then less likely to occur. The idea of organized hypocrisy suggests that organizations, in order to maintain flexibility, tend to decouple talk, decisions and practice. On the one hand, talk may facilitate legitimacy and certain decisions may satisfy specific interest groups. On the other hand, practice may be about getting things done without bothering too much about legitimacy and making decisions to satisfy various interest groups that are not likely to know or even care about how things actually work in practice (Meyer and Rowan, 1977).

Ultimately, a contribution that is seen as really interesting includes something that clearly stands out and is challenging and provocative. The innovate nature of not only the cognitive labor but also the work of crafting of the text must be emphasized. Writing is always important, and definitively so also for research that aims to create new, surprising assumptions. It is probably more important to think creatively about writing in this kind of work than in most incremental, add-to-the-established-literature kind of research, often calling for the adaptation of a conventional writing style.

5. Considering assumptions in relation to the audience

Assumptions to be targeted for challenge must be considered in relation to the groups who hold them and the general intellectual, social and political situation of a research community. This is a complex issue because the 'audience' is typically not a unitary group – primarily because there is often not one but multiple audiences, and the assumptions held by one audience may differ from the assumptions held by another audience. It is also likely that one particular audience consists of several sub-groups, which makes it even harder to specify the potentially relevant audiences. For instance, within a specific area, such as consumer studies or even interpretive consumer studies, there is an ambiguous mass of overlapping groups, which are difficult to separate into clear segments.

A possible relevant group to consider in evaluating an alternative assumption ground is research funding bodies, as these often consist of a mix of specialist, broader academic and general policy/public interest concerns. Funding bodies can then be seen as a form of proxy or indicator of those who are supposed to be finding the research contribution valuable and interesting. Additionally, policymakers and administrators, more generally, may be central.

Moving outside one's, sometimes overspecialized, sub-field makes it more difficult to know the assumptions of a possible broader audience. Professional and layperson audiences may be even harder to identify and delimit since they are usually not as well documented as academic audiences. One option could be to review the more popular professional magazines that practitioners read and perhaps also write for. Apart from literature reviews, it is also important to talk and listen to both academics and, when relevant, practitioners and others in order to understand their views of the particular subject matter in question and the assumptions they hold about it. Mass media and talking with neighbors, relatives, friends and other 'civilians' can give indications of more broadly shared assumptions, although the diversity here is huge and the assumptions of the general public may be of less interest when it comes to generating an interesting theoretical contribution. However, in most cases researchers wanting to challenge assumptions do not primarily target lay audiences. But it is of course a significant advantage if one can generate an appeal beyond a small group of fellow academics and potentially have something interesting to say to a broader spectrum of the educated public, including then academics outside one's own sub-field. Many research topics within social science are of potential interest to a large public and/or professional audience.

Sometimes a closer investigation or consideration of the expectations and assumptions of the audience leads to revisions of the entire project, including the literature domain one started with and the assumptions targeted for challenge.

It is also important to recognize the politics involved when choosing the assumptions to be challenged. It is a matter not only of advancing science but also of understanding research politics – who will lose or win when a specific assumption is challenged? Similarly, what type of challenge can an audience accept cognitively and emotionally? In other words, how can assumptions be challenged without upsetting dominant groups so much that they ignore the critique or even prevent one's study from being published? Here the problematization of in-house and root metaphor assumptions will probably be received more positively (less defensively) than the problematization of ideology, paradigm or field assumptions. But one can also consider the risk of *not* upsetting somebody. Consensus-breaking work should also clearly come through as such, and confrontation may be vital in order to create a desired reader effect.

One could add that an acceptance of an alternative assumption ground is not necessarily an objective or important consideration of the researcher. One approach is to be quite undiplomatic and more bluntly provocative. This can be productive and make the contribution even more interesting, at least for certain segments of the audience. If the ambition, however, is to produce what is viewed as interesting for an audience that strongly holds an alternative view of the subject matter from the one suggested, a 'balance' between challenging some of the audience's assumptions and leaving others 'undisturbed' is important. There needs to be a dialogical element in the contribution, connecting with the worldview of the audience and considering the risk of the latter shutting itself off from what you propose.

In order to accomplish the intended effect of surprise, challenge and opening up to the unexpected it is therefore crucial to consider readers' responses. A commonly used rhetorical strategy is politeness (Myers, 1993). For instance, all the authors in the texts investigated by Locke and Golden-Biddle (1997) used various politeness strategies (such as acknowledging other researchers for their contribution to the field) to reduce the risk of upsetting the academics they were (mildly) criticizing. Assumption-challenging should, of course, not overdo this or exaggerate similarities with existing work. A key element is the *challenge* of assumptions and this calls for punch. But one can, in order to moderate the 'shock effect' (if there is one) and maintain preparedness, point to commonalities and the acceptance of a certain common intellectual ground with the elements of consensus-breaking.

It is also possible to pay more or less attention to the assumptions to be challenged in relationship to novel, alternative assumptions. One may carefully and extensively deliver a critique against dominating thinking in an area, pointing to problematic beliefs in influential and/or representative texts. Alternatively, one may pay less attention to this in one's text and instead more pointedly emphasize the alternative assumption ground. The degree of critique may thus be more or less salient. For example, one may make a strong case for why the new assumption ground is clearly superior or one may take more of a pluralistic stance and point out a few alternative assumptions to be considered. Some critique is always needed, but whether one takes a 'what is basically wrong with this' or 'can we think differently about this issue' approach leads to rather different developments of the project.

Other tactics and writing styles, involving more of a confrontation, are also possible. In such tactics less attention to similarities and appeals to a 'we' with the audience is involved. Perhaps more assumptions are challenged and/or one focuses exclusively on these, making the consensus-confirming/-challenging ratio different from the 'balancing', confirming common ground-view. This issue is partly based on one's contribution – it may involve something that is more or less radically new – but is also very much a matter of choice of writing style.

6. Evaluating the alternative assumption ground

Following the body of work focusing on interestingness in theory development (Bartunek et al., 2006; Davis, 1971; McKinley et al., 1999), the ultimate indicator of whether problematization is going to be successful is not so much rigor and empirical support – although these qualities are always part of the picture – as the experience of 'this is interesting.' Davis (1971) suggests three responses (see Figure 5.2) that can be used to evaluate to what extent an alternative assumption ground is likely to generate a theory that will be regarded as interesting.

That's obvious! If the set of alternative assumptions to a large extent confirms the assumptions held by the targeted audiences – what they already assume to be the case about the subject matter – many will regard it as obvious.

That's absurd! If, however, the alternative assumption ground denies all the assumptions held by the targeted audiences, it is likely that it will be regarded as unbelievable. Both of the above responses indicate that the alternative assumption ground is likely to be unsuccessful.

That's interesting! This is the ideal response. According to Davis and other advocates of 'interesting theories' (Weick, 1989), the experience of 'this is interesting'

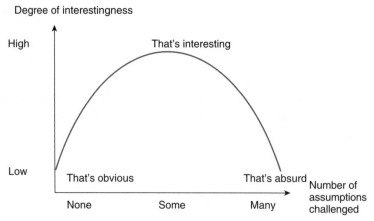

Figure 5.2 *Indicator of the interestingness of a research contribution*

occurs when the alternative assumption ground accepts some and denies some of the assumptions held by the targeted audiences. Because they are curious and willing to listen, the audiences may take the new idea or challenge seriously. Hence, the litmus test for being considered interesting is that the alternative assumption ground should fall somewhere between what is regarded as obvious and absurd.

A significant problem is audience diversity and audience fragmentation. Some areas are more homogeneous, others are diverse, changing and also messy as boundaries are loose and a lot of people are moving in or out or are on the periphery. So writing a contribution may lead to all the possible responses coming from different audiences. In some instances this leads to a morass of conflicting reviews with no clear direction and little chance of acceptance for journal publication. More often it leads to a narrow focus and the sub-specialization of academic work – intertwined with gap-spotting, which is evident in much contemporary research in the social sciences. Audience responses to such narrow academic work are then easier, but often with the loss of whether the research is really interesting and even more so if it will be influential.

One could add to the intellectual response revolving around novelty, surprise and excitement (Abbott, 2004), that it is important to consider the perceived fruitfulness or relevance of the new research question for developing new research programs and for contributing new knowledge having social relevance (Corley and Gioia, 2011; Van de Ven, 2007). Additionally, it may also be important to take into account an audience's response to the complexity of an alternative assumption (Peter and Olson, 1986). For example, if the alternative assumption ground is very complex, the response from the audience targeted may be less enthusiastic as it needs to devote considerable time to grasp and use the proposed assumption ground. Conversely, if the alternative assumption ground is simpler but still powerful, the response is likely to be more positive as its audiences can grasp and use it without too much effort. This is a matter of the payoff of the knowledge contribution for the audience.

It is important as well to test the alternative assumption ground on various representatives from the targeted audiences. How do they react? Considering such reactions over time is important. Initial responses may differ from later ones. Sometimes what immediately appears to be a novel and interesting alternative assumption may not hold water after critical scrutiny. In other cases, there may at first be a lukewarm or even cold response – or even total disinterest – but gradually that may change. Some of the most influential writings in social science have only been published after many years of unsuccessful attempts.

Developments in audiences' responses to an alternative assumption over time can also be important to consider in problematization. A gradual learning process may lead to further work with the project, developing interesting knowledge. Assumptions may be revised and developed, new forms of rhetoric may be introduced, and alternative publication outlets and various core audiences (sometimes associated with specific journals targeted) may be approached. Since so much has been said already and audiences will often respond in unexpected ways (or, more commonly will not respond at all), we can never be sure about the brilliance of our ideas. We therefore constantly need to take seriously what people find to be interesting (or not).

Conclusion

In this chapter we have developed a framework, a problematization methodology for challenging assumptions underlying the existing literature with the purpose of generating research questions that may increase the possibility of their resulting in imaginative, interesting and – thus – influential research projects and results. More specifically we have elaborated a typology that specifies which assumptions are open to problematization and a set of principles for identifying, articulating and challenging the assumptions underlying existing literature. Such assumption challenging calls for hermeneutic in-depth studies of texts in order to interpret assumptions, a careful assessment of these, and good judgment for choosing worthy and interesting assumptions to be challenged, as well as creative efforts to formulate alternative assumptions leading to the experience 'this is interesting'. Our hope is that the framework will help researchers to avoid reproducing established and dominant taken-for-granted assumptions and instead construct research questions that are consensus-challenging and novel. This will increase the chance of developing less predictable and boring research projects and theories than those which the majority of social scientists seem to produce today. The outlined problematization methodology is summarized in Table 5.1 below.

However, instead of trying to adhere strictly to our proposed methodology it is more important to reflect critically upon and avoid the uncritical or lazy reproduction of mainstream views within a field. We see the ideas in this book as inspiring and exemplifying an intellectual orientation towards working with assumptions and developing new ideas and research questions. The suggested methodology should therefore not be read as 'take it or leave it', but as a resource to use, to develop or vary – or as an invitation to challenge and come up with another and perhaps better one. It is important to recognize that challenging assumptions is very much a matter

Table 5.1 *Problematization methodology and its key elements*

Aim of the problematization methodology

Generating novel research questions through a *dialectical interrogation* of one's own familiar position, other stances, and the literature domain targeted for assumption challenging

A typology of assumptions open for problematization

In-house: Assumptions that exist within a specific school of thought	Root metaphor: Broader images of particular subject matter underlying existing literature	Paradigm: Ontological, epistemological, and methodological assumptions underlying existing literature	Ideology: Political-, moral-, and gender-related assumptions underlying existing literature	Field: Assumptions about a specific subject matter that are shared across different theoretical schools

Principles for identifying and challenging assumptions

1. Identify a domain of literature: What main bodies of literature and key texts make up the domain?	2. Identify and articulate assumptions: What major assumptions underlie the literature within the identified domain?	3. Evaluate articulated assumptions: Are the identified assumptions worthy to be challenged?	4. Develop alternative assumptions: What alternative assumptions can be developed?	5. Relate assumptions to audience: How can one craft a convincing message to the major audiences that hold the challenged assumptions?	6. Evaluate alternative assumptions: Are the alternative assumptions likely to generate a theory that will be regarded as interesting by the audiences targeted?

of creative and imaginative work. But some overall suggestions for key elements and steps to consider may facilitate innovation. Research is almost never solely about getting divine inspiration or relying on one's creative genius. Most of us typically also need to be systematic and methodological in what we do.

In Chapter 6 we will illustrate how the problematization methodology can be used for constructing research questions by applying it to two concrete areas in social science, namely identity in organizations and the (un)doing of gender. Again, although it is important to underscore that researchers engaged in problematization processes can follow a variety of routes and use different tricks and resources in order to challenge assumptions, for illustrative purposes we broadly follow the six problematization principles outlined above sequentially.

6

APPLYING THE PROBLEMATIZATION METHODOLOGY IN PRACTICE

In Chapter 5, we proposed and elaborated on problematization as a methodology for generating more interesting and innovative research questions by identifying and challenging the assumptions underlying existing literature. We first outlined a typology that specified which types of assumptions are open to problematization. Thereafter we developed a set of principles for identifying and challenging assumptions and, based on that, constructing novel research questions that potentially can lead to high-impact studies.

The purpose of this chapter is to illustrate concretely how the problematization methodology can be used to generate research questions from a specific body of literature. In order to provide a rich and detailed illustration of how it can be used in practice we have limited our application to two different established theories, namely Dutton et al.'s (1994) study of identity in organizations and West and Zimmerman's (1987) study of the (un-)doing of gender. Both are influential studies that are frequently cited and have informed quite a lot of research. (According to Google Scholar, at the time of writing, Dutton et al. has garnered about 2000 citations and West and Zimmerman, being a somewhat older study, has received well over 4000 citations.)

Dutton et al.'s (1994) study is from the organization studies field and concerns the identities of organizations and employees' identification with their workplaces. West and Zimmerman's (1987) study cuts across disciplines and investigates the understanding of gender and its formation in society. Below we illustrate how the problematization methodology can be used to identify and challenge assumptions in these two established theories and, based on doing so, to construct and formulate research questions that open up new and novel areas of inquiry.

Again, while the actual problematization process is considerably more organic, for illustrative purposes we follow the six problematization principles outlined in Chapter 5 sequentially, that is: (1) identifying a domain of literature, (2) identifying and articulating the assumptions underlying this domain, (3) evaluating these, (4) developing an alternative assumption ground, (5) considering it in relation to its audience and (6) evaluating an alternative assumption ground. But to re-emphasize what we said in the previous chapter, the problematization methodology is not mainly or necessarily about adhering strictly to certain procedures and rules. It is intended to express and encourage a particular intellectual attitude and ambition. The proof of the pudding is in the generation of innovative questions that lead to interesting and influential theories, not in following a methodological procedure slavishly. However, thoroughness and diligence in searching for, examining and rethinking assumptions may be very helpful in this rather difficult enterprise. For the creative genius this may not be so important, but for the rest of us it may be very helpful, indeed necessary.

Example 1: Problematizing identity in organizations

1. Identifying a domain of literature for assumption-challenging investigations

In order to illustrate our problematization methodology on the subject matter 'identity in organizations', we choose to focus primarily on Dutton et al.'s (1994) path-setting study, 'Organizational images and member identification', within the domain of identity constructions in organizations. Although focusing on a key text offers a good opportunity for an in-depth exploration of assumptions, it can also lead to limited results. Therefore, in order to accomplish a broader relevance, we also consider a few other influential studies in the domain with a somewhat different approach.[1] There is also a wealth of other studies that, to various degrees, are relevant in problematizing Dutton's et al.'s text.[2] However, in order to focus on the elements in the problematization methodology, with the exception of a few occasions, we avoid looking at how others have raised points of relevance for discussing the various issues that we address in our problematization of Dutton et al.'s text below.

The particular subject matter in Dutton et al.'s study is how individuals are attached to social groups, which they conceptualize as 'member identification'. They explain it as follows:

> Members vary in how much they identify with their work organization. When they identify strongly with the organization, the attributes they use to define the organization also define them. Organizations affect their members through this identification process, as shown by the comments of a 3M salesman, quoted in Garbett (1988: 2): 'I found out today that it is a lot easier being a salesman for 3M than for a little jobber no one has ever heard of. When you don't have to waste time justifying your existence or explaining why you are here, it gives you a certain amount of self-assurance. And I discovered I came across warmer and friendlier. It made me feel good and enthusiastic to be "somebody" for a change.' This salesman attributes his new, more positive sense of self to his membership in 3M, a well-known company. What he thinks about his organization and what he suspects others think about his organization affects the way that he thinks about himself as a salesperson. (1994: 239)

---

[1] See for example Ashforth and Mael (1989), Gioia et al. (2000), Pratt (2000) and Pratt and Foreman (2000).
[2] See for example Alvesson et al. (2008), Brown (2006), Collinson (2003), Deetz (1992), Elsbach (1999), Foucault (1977, 1980), Haslam (2004), Jenkins (2000), Knights and Willmott (1989), Shotter and Gergen (1989) and Weedon (1987).

Dutton et al. try to understand member identification by investigating how 'a member's cognitive connection with his or her work organization … [derives] from images that each member has of the organization' (1994: 239). The first image (what the member believes is distinctive, central and enduring about the organization) is defined as perceived organizational identity. The second image (what the member believes outsiders think about the organization) is called 'the construed external image' (1994: 239). Dutton et al. develop a model of member identification that suggests that the two organizational images 'influence the cognitive connection that members create with their organization and the kind of behaviors that follow' (1994: 239). Their model proposes 'members assess the attractiveness of these images by how well the image preserves the continuity of their self-concept, provides distinctiveness, and enhances self-esteem' (1994: 239). Based on the model, they develop a range of propositions about organizational identification. These can be tested, but here we look at the assumptions behind the propositions.

2. Identifying and articulating the assumptions underlying the chosen domain of literature

Although Dutton et al. point out explicitly that a central assumption of their study is that people's sense of membership in an organization shapes their self-conceptions; very few assumptions on which they base their argument are highlighted in this way. Instead, the text creates the impression that its argument and logic are grounded in specific factors reflecting self-evident truths. For example, the authors claim that a perceived organizational identity exists in the sense of a member's having beliefs about the distinctive, central and enduring attributes of the organization (reflecting Albert and Whetten's [1985] definition), and that an organizational member sometimes defines him/herself by the same attributes that he or she believes define the organization. But these statements contain assumptions that conceptualize their subject matter of how individuals are attached to organizations in a particular way and are not necessarily correct or productive.

Let us first consider the statement 'a member's beliefs about the distinctive, central, and enduring attributes of the organization' (Dutton et al. 1994: 239). One of its assumptions is that people see themselves as members of an organization, as if the latter is like a club or an association, which people join as a positive choice. Another is that members have beliefs about attributes of the organization and that these attributes are distinctive, central and enduring. Similarly, the statement 'the degree to which a member defines him- or herself by the same attributes that he or she believes define the organization' (1994: 239) is also underpinned by a range of assumptions. One is that individuals and organizations are constituted by a set of inherent and more or less stable attributes. Another is that the attributes of the individual are comparable with the attributes of the organization through a member's cognitive connection. Based on those assumptions, Dutton et al. conceptualize person and organization as externally related to each other through an individual's images of his or her organization and what outsiders think about the organization. This reasoning carries a range of paradigmatic assumptions, such as the dualist ontological assumption that a person and the world exist independent of each other (Sandberg and Targama, 2007: ch. 2).

Let us briefly compare the Dutton et al. text with the other selected texts in the domain. Pratt (2000), drawing heavily on Dutton et al., investigated 'how organizations attempt, succeed, and fail to change how members view themselves in relation to the organization' (2000: 457). His work departs from the emphasis in the literature that 'most research [should] focus on how organizations successfully engender strong ties with members' and instead should 'look at organizational conditions that lead to positive, negative, ambivalent and broken identifications' (2000: 457), and at how identification management is 'associated with a variety of identification types' (2000: 458).

While sharing similar assumptions as Dutton et al., Pratt adds to the literature by pointing out that the individual can change identification states. His claim resonates to some extent with Ashforth's claim that 'identity is perpetual work in progress' (1998: 213), further underscored by Ashforth and Mael's observation of 'the often unique and context-specific demands of an identity' (1989: 147). In a similar vein, Gioia et al. argue that the 'apparent durability of identity is somewhat illusory' (2000: 64), because it is mainly a matter of 'the stability used by organization members to express what they believe the organization to be' (2000: 64). Hence, while still sharing Dutton et al.'s assumptions that organizational member identification is a 'distinctive and enduring characteristic' (Ashforth and Mael, 1989: 154), the above authors express a more dynamic and less organization-focused view of organizational identification.

The assumptions held by Dutton et al. (and to a significant degree also by Ashforth and Mael, Gioia et al. and Pratt) can be further elaborated and articulated with the help of the assumptions typology. For example, their assumption that members may have beliefs about the specific attributes of the organization can be regarded as an in-house assumption among these authors. The assumption that individuals are carriers of beliefs can also be targeted at a paradigmatic level. The 'natural' and potentially harmonious relationship between individuals and the (humanlike) organization indicated by the overlap of characteristics can be further explored in terms of ideology. The very idea that there is something – constructed or not – such as 'organizational identity' or 'individual identity' and that they are worthy of investigation may indicate some field-level assumptions.

3. Evaluating articulated assumptions

The assumptions identified above (on membership, fixed perceptions of the individual and the organization as a thing-like phenomenon, and a perceived similarity between individual and organizational attributes) need to be assessed to determine if, and to what extent, they are worthy of further problematizations. For example, the assumption that people regard themselves as members of their work organizations can be challenged with the more instrumental and often darker aspects of employment. One can thus question Dutton et al.'s ideological assumption of an 'organizational man' view of a positive and strong link between an employer and a compliant employee with a limited independent self, using the employment situation as a natural and significant source of identity. Pratt's (2000) work opens this up to some extent by pointing out less positive identifications, but it still adheres to the assumption that 'members view themselves in relation to the organization' and that issues around identity 'can and should be managed' (Pratt and Foreman, 2000: 18).

The assumption that members have beliefs about attributes of the organization and that these attributes are distinctive, central and enduring can also be further questioned. Are people's ways of relating to organizations typically so thing-like? Using an alternative metaphor, the organization can perhaps be seen as a broad and complex terrain in which perceptions and sentiments shift, depending on aspects, moments and contexts. For example, 'organization' may sometimes refer to colleagues or to top management; at other times to one's own department or work or one's future career prospects, rewards and fringe benefits; and, on other occasion, to mass media representations, products and HRM policies. As Ashcraft and Alvesson (2011) show, people construct and relate to a seemingly straightforward object like 'management' in highly shifting and varied ways. As an identification target, 'the organization' may be best conceived as multiple and moving. This is also to some extent pointed out by Gioia et al. (2000) and Pratt and Foreman (2000), but these authors still assume the existence of beliefs about the organization as a whole (and its central, distinct and enduring characteristics), while a counter-assumption could be that such an entity is not what most people primarily relate to.

The assumption that individuals and organizations hold similar attributes and generate a 'fit' appears to be as problematic and can be further questioned. The possible connection may be considerably more frictional, volatile and fluid. Ideas of varied identification types (Pratt, 2000), pluralistic beliefs about organizational identity (Pratt and Foreman, 2000), and identity changes reflecting image changes (Gioia et al., 2000) are also relevant to consider here, since they give some clues about which assumptions are worthwhile to problematize further.

4. Developing an alternative assumption ground

We now arrive at the task of developing counter assumptions, or at least alternatives, to the ones identified and articulated through the problematization above. Similar to the identification and articulation of the above assumptions, we can here draw on different theoretical positions to play up reference points and resources for problematization. One possible stance is critical theory, which provides at least two alternative assumptions. One proposes that the organizational membership assumption is a naive idealization of contemporary work experiences in flexible capitalism, strongly downplaying lasting relationships and commitment (Sennett, 1998) and thereby making organizational identification a rare or fragile phenomenon – perhaps a managerial dream rather than something existing on a broader scale. Another, and quite different, critical theory assumption is that the possibility of strong identification with the organization may mean people become cultural dopes and lose a clear sense of independence in relation to the employer, who wins the minds and hearts of employees (Kunda, 1992; Willmott, 1993).

A very different route would be to proceed from the economic man assumption about rational maximization of self-interest (Camerer and Fehr, 2006; Henrich et al., 2005), leading to a view of identification as a tactical resource for self-promotion. A third alternative would be to be influenced by a poststructuralist stance, in which the assumption of the organization as a fixed and one-dimensional object can be challenged by a hyper process or fluidity view of organizations as multidimensional, shape shifting and discursively constituted – a domain exhibiting multiple and varied social identities (Chia, 2000). This assumption is different from positions mainly pointing out changes over time (as expressed, for example, by Gioia et al., 2000, and Pratt, 2000).

The above problematizations, associated with (two versions of) critical theory, economic man thinking and radical process thinking, offer reference points for alternative assumptions. We selectively use all of these in order to develop novel research questions. As emphasized, problematization is best accomplished through using (but not directly applying) a broad set of theoretical stances, offering resources for unpacking and rethinking.

The assumption that postulates a stable and robust degree of perceived similarity between individual and organization could be related to ideas on variation, process and dynamics around self-definition and the construction of the organization. The possible *meeting points* – spaces for establishing a possible 'perceived similarity' – may be rare, since most parts of people's working lives may go on without them comparing themselves to the employing organization at a more abstract and holistic level. Still, these meeting points may be important. Rather than seeing the similarity between individual and organization as static (or only gradually dynamic, i.e. evolving as Pratt and Gioia et al. do), one can regard organization and individual as the different *traffic of stories* (of self and organization), and sometimes these stories may converge – that is, organizational identification temporarily occurs.

One possibility here could be that employees articulate a positive link between themselves and their organizations when the context implies certain advantages but not when it implies disadvantages. Identification is, thus, driven by self-interest, a discursive act and typically temporal and situation specific, sometimes opportunistic. Dutton et al.'s citation of the 3M employee above illustrates this. Since it can be an advantage to be a representative of a large and well-known firm in a certain sale situation, making presentation easier, a positive link between individual and organization is emphasized in that situation. Whether the same positive link – and identification – is expressed when corporate bureaucracy or hierarchy (often mentioned as negative aspects of very large firms), or performance pressure from management, provides the context is perhaps more doubtful. Possible identifications may therefore be more area specific and dynamic, existing in a space that also includes salient moments of alienation or opportunism. Research questions on the perceived unity or multi-contextuality of an organization (*if* that category is relevant for people) and how individuals may couple/decouple themselves at various times and in various domains (settings) may then be suggested.

Let us sum up alternative assumptions and research questions. First, people working in organizations more commonly see themselves as employees with varying experiences of organizational membership. An employee's way of defining him/herself may be more or less congruent, non-related to or antagonistic towards the meanings used to portray and refer to the organization. Do people see a similarity between themselves and their organization, and if so, how often and when? Perhaps the (rare?) situations in which statements of self and organization seem to be related can be explored as situation specific construction processes, offering sites for identity work.

Second, employees do not necessarily have fixed or enduring beliefs that change only slowly over time as an effect of radically new circumstances, as proposed by Gioia et al. (2000) and Pratt (2000). Instead, employees take temporary positions on their organizational affiliation, such as variations in their feelings about membership, being part of an employment contract and being subordinated to an organizational structure. Perhaps situation, event and process matter more than static or enduring images about attributes? Do people have/express consistent and united or shifting and fragmented beliefs/images about self and organization? One can here imagine a garbage can-like situation, in which the individual and various social identities and identification options (organizational but also group, occupational, ethnic, gender and age) plus various subject positions (for example, opportunism, alienation, sense of belonging) are mixed together and come together in a variety of combinations. Occasionally, a positive construction of organizational identity becomes linked to a positive self-conception through identification, but perhaps this is a temporal, fragile and possibly rare position rather than a fixed trait?

5. Considering assumptions in relation to the audience

The four previous principles indicate reasons to reconsider some of the assumptions underlying not only Dutton et al.'s approach but also broader parts of the organizational identity and identification domain. A key assumption in this large and expanding literature domain (Haslam and Reicher, 2006) is that most employees define themselves as organizational members or they may, given proper (identity) management, do so. This can, of course, motivate various forms of problematization – ranging from the strong (paradigmatic), aiming at undermining the key belief that people define themselves partly or mainly through belonging to an organization (in terms of central, distinctive and enduring traits), as indicated by the organizational identity and identification industry, to the milder, suggesting revisions through more limited (in-house) problematizations.

On the one hand, given the heavy research investment and the structuring of organization studies partly around identity as a key sub-field and a key variable, a strong problematization case may be seen as irrelevant (absurd) and become marginalized. On the other hand, a radical challenge of conventional identity research may be applauded by various groups that hold more process-sensitive social constructionist assumptions about identification, although they may not regard these as particularly novel. However, being taken seriously by the majority of management scholars and practitioners probably implies a less extreme version than that favored by poststructuralists, which we think our alternative assumption ground expresses. Also, within the group whose assumptions are challenged, a variety of responses can be expected. Some of these will no doubt be political, since researchers have vested interests in and identify with their theories (Bourdieu, 2004; Breslau, 1997).

6. Evaluating the alternative assumption ground

The main task of the sixth problematization principle is to assess to what extent the alternative assumption ground can lead to new research questions that have the potential to generate more interesting identity theories. A first step in such an evaluation is to further explore which major audiences are related to the identity field within organization theory and, perhaps, also more broadly in the social sciences. While it does not seem worthwhile to do so here, a review of existing literature on identity in organizations would be central for identifying major audience segments, since it would offer material on how to fine-tune the message. Even without reviewing the existing literature in detail, an important audience in our example is likely to be those who broadly share (consciously or unconsciously) the cognitive psychology perspective on which Dutton et al.'s work is based, together with those favoring a view of the world made up by perceptions of stable entities. It is also important to note that the response from advocates of a cognitive psychology perspective may vary depending on what particular discipline is targeted, such as psychology, social psychology, sociology or organization studies.

When the major audiences are known, we are in a position to use the criteria suggested by Davis. Will they regard the alternative assumption ground as absurd, irrelevant, or interesting and promising? Although the alternative assumption ground suggests that individuals' identification with organizations is far more weak (or even non-existent), fluid and volatile than is assumed by Dutton et al. (and, on the whole, by many other influential organizational identification researchers as well), it does not robustly question the conceptualization of the subject matter, member identification, as such. Nor does the alternative set of assumptions provide a deliberate ground attack on the paradigmatic assumptions underlying the cognitive perspective adopted by Dutton et al. It is therefore possible that the alternative set of assumptions will be found to be potentially interesting by many of the audiences addressing organizational identity and identification from a functionalist viewpoint.

The extent to which more radical social constructionist audiences will find our alternative assumptions interesting is questionable, since they already embrace some of them. If they were targeted, the task would be to avoid the 'that's obvious' response, perhaps by emphasizing the continuation and development of a particular line of thought (not in itself targeted for problematization). For this audience the problematization of a quite different set of assumptions from those of the Dutton et al. text is relevant.

If the alternative assumption ground is likely to be regarded as interesting by our targeted audiences, we are in a position to leave the problematization process and begin to formulate new research questions. For example, do employees construct/perceive their employing organizations in stable ways? And, if so, when and in what ways, if any, would the personal meaning be related to (varieties of) self-identity of these possible constructions/perceptions? One could possibly sharpen this question further. Rather than assuming that employees are members with clear and, over at least a short time period, fixed beliefs about organizational distinctiveness and endurance, one could proceed from the idea that they are (normally) not best conceptualized as members and could study *if*, *when*, *why* and *how* people construct themselves as members having fixed beliefs about their employing organizations in relationship to themselves. The study of the circulation of self and organizational representations/identity possibilities and garbage can-like connections and disconnections could be an interesting research task. For example, do people move and, if so, how between identification as a positive and a negative source of social identity and to what extent are such moves driven by calculative and exploitative motives and experience of skeptical distancing (de-identification)?

Studying how employees arrive at and maintain beliefs that their organizations have traits that are distinctive, central and enduring could also be a useful research task. Being able to produce a coherent set of such beliefs would not be seen as unproblematic and typical but as a true accomplishment, facilitated by an ability to block out the changing, ambiguous and fragmented nature of contemporary organizational life. Assuming a fluid and non-reified nature of social reality, organizational identity and self-identity, as well as alignment constructions ('I am similar to my organization'), could be viewed as a de-fragmentation and de-processualization of organizational life, countering the multiple and moving constructions of the themes included. Interesting, problematization-based research questions could then be formulated as follows: Do people stabilize themes like organization and self and organizational/self-identification? What are the (rare) conditions and operations under which experiences of self and organization can be cognitively frozen and symbolically merged? Alternatively expressed, when and how do positive stories of self and organization happily merge? The production of organizational identity as a topic and the more or less taken-for granted phenomenon of such identification are then placed in a dynamic and fluid context. And the specific construction processes involved are then opened up for inquiry.

Would these research questions lead to more interesting and influential research than a study building positively on Dutton et al.? There are no guarantees, but if all the research on this topic, as referred to in Chapters 1 and 4, is right one could expect that the research questions generated through the problematization of assumptions underlying Dutton et al.'s approach are more likely to lead to an interesting theory than the use of a gap-spotting strategy to identify or create a gap in their approach that needs to be filled.

Example 2: Problematizing the (un-)doing of gender

1. Identifying a domain of literature for assumption-challenging investigations

Gender is a central theme within the social sciences, which has created a wealth of theory and research. It is generally seen as something socially and culturally defined rather than biologically determined, although there is a lot of complexity and debate around the sex/gender distinctions and the socially constructed nature of biological criteria. The field of gender studies is enormous and stretches over several disciplines, which makes it almost impossible to grasp. Here, we concentrate on one sociological key text in gender studies, namely West and Zimmerman's (1987) classic work 'Doing gender'. Their work seems to be well suited to an investigation of its underlying assumptions. First, their perspective is widely acknowledged and seen as path-setting within gender studies, leading to the majority of researchers within the school applying and (thus) confirming its assumptions (Deutsch, 2007). Second, the authors themselves, in a recent commentary (West and Zimmerman, 2009), see no reason to revise their original position. As our task in this chapter is to illustrate the problematization methodology, we only refer to a few other studies when they are of particular relevance for West and Zimmerman's work. (Examples here would include Alvesson and Billing, 2009; Butler, 2004; and Deutsch, 2007). Moreover, the aim is not to discuss a comprehensive set of gender aspects. Instead, the purpose is to show how novel research questions can be developed based on assumptions that are different from those underlying West and Zimmerman's doing gender school.

The particular subject matter in West and Zimmerman's (1987) study is how we do gender in interaction. Their aim is 'to explore how gender might be exhibited or portrayed through interaction, and thus be seen as "natural," while it is being produced as a socially organized achievement' (1987: 129). Hence, the authors conceptualize gender not as something biological or fixed but as an ongoing accomplishment that takes place in everyday interaction. Their gender doing perspective is based on ethnomethodology and draws on Garfinkel and Goffman but can also be seen as an original contribution that stands on its own.

West and Zimmerman take issue with a number of common theoretical views on gender, including the ideas that gender is a set of traits, a variable, a role or a structural characteristic. Instead, they see gender as 'the product of social doings of some sort' (1987: 129). That gender is not primarily biological but rather socially achieved is broadly recognized in gender studies. Sometimes this gender achievement is viewed as taking place through socialization leading to a gender identity. But according to West and Zimmerman, gender is not something that after a few years or even after a long-term socialization becomes fixed, unvarying or static. Rather, it is achieved through ongoing social interaction: it 'is a routine, methodical, and recurring accomplishment' (1987: 126). This more or less constantly ongoing accomplishment is guided by the pressure coming from institutionalized frameworks leading to expectations of appearing gender-appropriate. However, doing gender appropriately is not just a matter of fitting into a specific sex role but also calls for a complex set of situated responses. These include managing occasions 'so that, whatever the particulars, the outcome is seen and seeable in context as gender-appropriate or, as the case may be, gender-*in*appropriate, that is *accountable*' (1987: 135).

West and Zimmerman's work offers a distinct conceptualization of gender and has formed the basis for an intellectual tradition within gender studies, which almost exclusively focuses on gender doing as involving constraints and disadvantages for women (and to some extent men). As Deutsch (2007) shows, almost all work inspired by West and Zimmerman investigates how gender relations are maintained. The doing means complying and reproducing gender-appropriate ways of being. Even if people in some ways deviate from traditional gendered ways of being, studies inspired by the doing gender perspective tend to focus on how people still in various ways do gender in line with traditional conceptions and expectations. Females in managerial jobs, for example, exhibit certain forms of femininity in leadership/follower relations, dress or work–family balance. So even if people are not only, or mainly, being gender stereotypical, they are still engaged in significant elements of traditional gender maintenance, and this is what advocates of the gender doing perspective primarily focus on and investigate in their studies.

2. Identifying and articulating assumptions underlying the chosen domain of literature

'Doing gender' is in itself partly based on problematization, although perhaps of a programmatic type, as it is mainly informed by ethnomethodology. It challenges both the fairly fixed gender differences within socialization theories and structuralists' claims that structural arrangements, such as between work and family, define gender in specific ways. It draws upon works by Garfinkel and Goffman, but takes issue with Goffman about the nature of what the latter refers to as 'gender displays', that is, conventionalized portrayals of cultural beliefs and meanings of sex. While Goffman sees gender display as optional West and Zimmerman argue that it is non-optional in the sense that we are always seen by others as female or male and this leads to an enforced necessity of dealing with this, that is, to be engaged in constant gender doing. West and Zimmerman claim that the sex category of the actor 'attends virtually all actions' and raise the question if we can avoid doing gender and the answer is negative, 'doing gender is unavoidable' (1987: 145). The authors emphasize that 'participants in interaction organize their various and manifold activities to reflect or express gender, and they are disposed to perceive the behavior of others in a similar light' (1987: 127).

Some core assumptions underlying West and Zimmerman's doing gender perspective seem to be that:

1. gender is non-optional in the sense of an awareness that people are men or women and that a set of gender expectations is always in operation;
2. a key concern for people is the omnipresence of gender in the sense that they cannot neglect or downplay it;
3. how each of us is organizing and displaying our gender is closely scrutinized by others;

4 gender means something problematic in that it involves constant monitoring of possible deviations from 'normal' gender behavior and is thereby a source of constraint and inequality; and
5 gender is not primarily something individual but determined in social interaction.

Let us briefly support our claims that the above assumptions underlie West and Zimmerman's doing gender perspective.[3]

(1) The assumption that gender is non-optional relies on the idea that gender is not only in interaction, but also constantly on people's mind (as part of shared, homogeneous meanings guiding expectations) similar to the Freudian notion that sex is always on people's minds. In their recent commentary, West and Zimmerman (2009) explain that once members of a society have created distinctions among themselves, such as 'incumbents of different sex categories', they are 'used to affirm different category incumbents 'essentially different natures' and the institutional arrangements based on these' (2009: 114).

(2) Gender is omnipresent and constantly significant. According to West and Zimmerman, we are to be seen as men and women because 'one circumstance that attends virtually all actions is the sex category of the actor' (1987: 136). Although West and Zimmerman do not directly claim the significance of doing gender, it is strongly communicated in the article as a self-evident fact. Everything else is addressed as situated and, by comparison, fairly trivial or non-significant. The usual formulas associated with the significance of gender, such as gender intersecting with race and class, are hardly mentioned. (The authors, however, do that in later writings.) Their assumption is that gender is normally highly significant in terms of what people are doing and that they are accountable for their gender doings. The awareness of this accountability seems to be a key concern for all interactions.

(3) The authors' work is based on the assumption that there is a sort of mutual interest or aligned understanding between individuals doing gender. The individual, at least as a competent member of society, is engaged in organizing and displaying gender and others are preoccupied by scrutinizing this individual's gender doing. The motivation for the former appears to be partly in the anticipated interest of others. That we are accountable for our gender doings and the risk of others finding the doings illegitimate or in other ways normatively dissatisfying appears to be a key driver behind the constant doings of gender in interactions.

---

[3]In order to fully support our claims about assumptions, we would need to use up much more space quoting their text. We will refrain from excessively doing so for space reasons and to avoid making our text tedious. The criteria for good use of the problematization methodology are less about delivering a very precise problematization and getting all the assumptions 'right' – as some are implicit there is always an element of guesswork/ambiguity involved here – than to produce reasonably interesting and fruitful alternative assumptions inspiring new research questions. A problematization exercise is thus somewhat different from a 'pure' critical scrutiny.

(4) Gender is viewed as a source of constraints and risks. Although West and Zimmerman do not suggest standardized male and female behavior, but rather emphasize skillful maneuvering in the light of gender, they still assume that gender is an evaluative framework that sanctions deviating gender behavior. It is perhaps less of a strict prison than a potential trap, as inappropriate ways of gender doing may lead to sanctions following on from negative judgment: '... to "do" gender is not always to live up to normative conceptions of femininity or masculinity, it is to engage in behavior *at the risk of gender assessment*' (1987: 136). They also refer to 'the fact that others will judge and respond to us' (p. 140).

(5) Gender is outside people's minds. Gender doings without individuals are impossible, but gender is less about individuals' identity or agency and more about their behavior in interactions. Adoption of the perceptions of others appears much more central than individuals' personal identity constructions. In fact, subjectivity and identity is almost lost in the interaction, apart from people needing to do gender in a fairly skillful way and driven by an anxiety for failure to be accountable. However, West and Zimmerman also point out the self-regulating process when people 'monitor their own and others' conduct with regard to its gender implications' (1987: 142). The individual manifests as a watchtower scrutinizing others (and one's self-performance) and as a more or less skillful performer and deliverer of appropriate gender under the surveillance from others. On the whole, West and Zimmerman are constantly emphasizing interaction rather than identities, aspirations, motives, feelings, subjectivities and so on, leading to the assumption that gender is primarily out there – in interactions – and less (or hardly at all) in subjectivities. The impression is that when not being in an interaction, gender is not really an issue.

3. Evaluating articulated assumptions

All these assumptions offer interesting ideas and we think gender research based on these assumptions can be very productive. Our intention is not to discourage researchers from following the doing gender research program. But as the idea of producing interesting research questions through problematization suggests, investigating and challenging assumptions is a key driver behind novelty and after 25 years and hundreds of studies following in the footsteps of West and Zimmerman (Deutsch, 2007), the above assumptions can be evaluated critically in order to suggest new research avenues. We do not claim these are false, but rather than continue to reproduce them, it may be interesting to see if alternative assumptions may be interesting to work from.

Evaluating assumptions 1 and 2, is gender non-optional, omnipresent and constantly significant? While it is plausible that we never leave our bodies at home when we go out and regularly consider the gender of people we meet in interactions, this does not mean that sometimes gender cannot be optional or at least not be salient. Even if one typically notes the gender of the person one is interacting with, it is not given that it is done in a non-trivial sense. The assumption of the 'non-triviality of gender' relies on the idea that gender is not only a theme in (all) interaction, but also on people's minds. After all people do not act mindlessly. But perhaps not every interaction involves the doing of gender in a non-trivial way? People need to bring in anticipations and a normative framework about gender in order to make the doing of gender meaningful. Perhaps they (we) are not doing it all the time. Paying attention to gender may be highly variable. Sometimes (often, perhaps even very often) gender is 'there', the awareness of this being a man or woman is heightened, and the doing of gender is put in motion. But sometimes (perhaps less often) awareness of gender is on a lower, perhaps even trivial level. The doing of gender, even when there are visible elements of it in interaction, may thus be more or less significant.

There are areas, interaction types and issues that resonate with cultural ideas of masculinity and femininity in a specific society, but there are also situations that most people would normally view as fairly gender-neutral. Watching heavy porn or hunting, and knitting and taking care of small infants may be viewed as occasions for doing gender. But watching television news, preparing a meal, driving children to school, writing an academic article and talking about the weather with neighbors may be situations where gender doing is less or non-significant.[4] For example, journal editors, reviewers and colleagues do perhaps expect that when male and female academics engage in journal publication work they are not doing gender in West and Zimmerman's sense. This is not to say that there are not gendered norms in academia or in publication. Norms about writing in a highly analytical, abstract, impersonal way may be seen as an expression of middle-class, academic masculinity. But it is seldom expected that female authors display a particular notion of their femininity in journal texts accounting for their normality in relationship to a demand for accountability. Most journals would probably prevent authors from writing texts exhibiting doing gender in West and Zimmerman's sense. To suggest a kind of 'quasi-essential' presence of the doing of gender as a fixed ingredient in interaction can thus be questioned.

Evaluating assumption 3, does gender take place in a mutual compliance interest between individuals? West and Zimmerman assume there is a kind of generalized symmetry in social interaction in the sense that when an individual is doing gender in interaction with others, the others are inclined to assess the individual's gender doing negatively if it does not meet their expectations of gender-appropriateness. West and Zimmerman do not claim that other people always assess our gender doing. But the impression is that they think it is likely that one will be judged according to normative standards for one's gender category. All action is then informed by the risk of being evaluated by these norms and this forces individuals to constantly do gender. On the whole, there is a balance here: acting and judging lead people to typically do gender in a conformist way.

---

[4] Notice that we write 'may' here, that is, we are not making firm truth claims, but only want to open up to considerations and empirical inquiries on the possible non-significant gender nature of some activities. Of course, everything can be seen as gendered; cooking is (or was) female (as long it is not a matter of chefs or a barbecue), as is accompanying children to school, and so on. But the idea that everything is automatically defined as masculine and feminine may reflect the fixed convictions of researchers more than an open mind about how various groups may relate to gender norms and categories (Alvesson and Billing, 2009).

One could dispute such a generic symmetry. Perhaps there are often quite varied views of gender between different parties, such as variation in concerns and anxiety as well as an interest in, and likelihood of, giving gender assessments. Assuming considerable pluralism and fragmentation in contemporary Western society, any anticipation of a uniform gendered normative framework seems questionable. There are domains where these exist, but the fear of deviating is hardly straightforward and the risk may be mild or never anticipated or negative assessments may simply not be picked up. Normative frameworks may also go against 'doing gender' in a conventional manner like sanctioning people for acting in gender stereotypical ways.

There is a complex network of meanings that encourages us to adapt to, and at the same time liberate ourselves from, traditional and sometimes old-fashioned frameworks that are still sometimes in use. The idea that women who engage in sport and men who engage in childcare and so on must demonstrate their femininity and masculinity, cannot be taken for granted. Even when they do (which a lot of research demonstrates) these doings may be minor (but possibly exaggerated by some researchers following the 'doing gender' path) compared to more significant elements of the doings (associated with class, ethnicity, professionalism, age, individuality or something else). However, the individuals who are supposed to comply with gendered normative frameworks and others who are supposed to carry out the gender assessment may be less concerned about gender. Furthermore, the assumed symmetry of doing gender in a smooth, gender-reproductive, interaction may not be particularly salient either. Interaction may be much more diverse and messy than is assumed by West and Zimmerman – including degrees of freedoms and failures of doing gender (without sanctions) or failures in gender doing (with sanctions from people disliking gender stereotypical behavior). All of this could significantly downplay inclinations to engage in the doing of gender.

Evaluating assumption 4, is gender a source of constraint and risk? For West and Zimmerman gender is a source of oppression, constraint, inequality and risk. Irrespective if one complies with or resists certain gender norms, risk is involved. Gender is then seen as a problem and appears to motivate people to conform (although this is often exercised in flexible and skillful ways through the use of a large number of resources for doing gender) because of uncertainty and the anxiety of being 'punished'. This conformism means 'interaction operates to sustain relations of inequality' (West and Zimmerman, 2009: 115).

Critics of gender doing have emphasized this negative side and the overemphasis on compliance and reproduction 'perpetuating the idea that the gender system of oppression is hopelessly impervious to real change' (Deutsch, 2007: 107). These critics point at variations in gender inequality that exist between and within societies, and over time. They also sometimes emphasize the radical changes that have happened, at least in most parts of Western societies over the recent decades, where gender relations today are quite different from a generation ago. Empirical studies of women's improved labor market situation during recent decades then offer input for problematization (McCall, 2005). Some authors use the expression 'un-doing' gender (Butler, 2004; Deutsch, 2007) as a way to highlight improvisation, resistance and change in gender doing. Here positive forces are emphasized. They still, however, tend to see gender as a problem, a prison-like arrangement, which you can resist and transform or within which you can carve out and use some space for freedom and creativity. However, one could here ask whether gender is only or mainly a problem, a source of risk and constraint. Perhaps there is something positive also about gender, even regarding gender doing. Perhaps more than risk-avoidance and heroic efforts to resist are involved.

Evaluating assumption 5, is gender always outside people's minds? The emphasis that gender is embedded in everyday interactions and therefore primarily 'outside' people and their internalized or fixed subjectivity means that gender is tightly connected to interactions and has no specific presence or inertia in people's subjective orientations. West and Zimmerman mention, 'gender identities that are important to individuals and that they strive to maintain' (1987: 142). But, on the whole, identities seem to be insignificant. Instead, it is the risk of being exposed to assessment and the need to be accountable that are the crucial elements in the gender doing perspective. One could, however, argue that gender identity is an important self-regulating mechanism even in the absence of interaction and the assessment of others. Gendered identity is not only about interpersonal interaction, it is also formed by media and socialization in the form of internalized ideas and self-perceptions that may be significant. As such gendered identity can function both as an input for interaction and as another source of doing (or undoing) of gender in various ways. One could for example see gender doing as something that individuals also do outside interactions and that gender doing in interactions is as much identity-determined as it is an outcome of the social control associated with the risk of negative sanctions.

One could perhaps add that empirical observations give the impression that people sometimes 'do gender' (act in gender stereotypical ways) despite the risk of disapproval from the environment in wanting them not to do it. For example, female professionals stay home and take care of children even though their managers may disapprove and people in the surrounding environment suggest that this is a gender trap and that the spouses should share the domestic work on a 50/50 basis. (This may sound odd in some countries and groups, but it is a norm in some places of the world.) Identity issues sometimes transcend normative assessments. One could here point to the relevance of using 'non-gender' theory, for example, with regard to organizational and professional effectiveness, inspiring the idea that at work people are sometimes assessed mainly on work performance and that this may lead to some 'non-doing' of gender.

Gender students often dismiss this kind of 'non-gender' literature as 'gender-blind', but it could still be used as a source for thinking differently about people at work from 'one-eyed' gender studies, seeing and emphasizing gender everywhere (Alvesson and Billing, 2009). Some research indicates that female and male managers do not differ much in leadership, and that there are elements in workplaces that at least downplay the prevalence of 'doing gender'. The evidence on whether females do leadership differently from their male counterparts is inconclusive (Alvesson and Billing, 2009; Cliff et al., 2005; Eagly and Johannesen-Schmidt, 2001). However, the very same evidence could be read as indicating that the pressure to do gender is not always so strong. This reading is supported by the possibility that if the pressure to do gender would be constantly strong there ought to be much clearer signs on gender differences in leadership. Perhaps other elements and contingencies in social life often matter more. Empirical leadership studies could then give some input to problematization.

4. Developing an alternative assumption ground

The next step is to formulate alternative assumptions based on the problematization of the identified assumptions underlying the gender doing perspective. It could be argued that gender is not constantly omnipresent and significant (assumptions 1 and 2), but varies in presence, meaning and significance. The cultural correlates of gender are almost endless and are invoked or bypassed in various ways and to various degrees. Just because a body is present does not automatically mean that a set of cultural standards around appropriate masculinity or femininity is put into operation. It is possible to imagine that sometimes only limited attention is paid to gender doing and the normative framework for assessing it. A starting point for an alternative inquiry could be that many situations and actions may *not* be viewed in terms of gender appropriateness. Possible questions for investigation become then *when* does gender doing occur and/or when is it significant?

An alternative to the idea that gender doing takes place in an alignment of shared meanings between individuals (assumption 3), could be to emphasize fragmentation and diversity. Here poststructuralism would be a resource for rethinking the idea of smoothness and universality in the doing of gender (Alvesson, 2002; Butler, 2004). It could be argued that there is no (at least not in the contemporary Western world) homogeneous framework of how to assess gender and that it is uniformly shared and enforced. The anxiety of being judged negatively in terms of gender may be strong, but it may vary a lot depending on people's interest, attentions and possible criteria for gender appropriateness. For example, a waitress may be less interested in appearing feminine compared to being seen as competent in giving good advice and getting the food and drink right. Similarly, a guest may pay more or less attention to femininity or to good advice and good delivery. It is also likely that both the waitress and the guest may misjudge each other's readings of the situation, but this may go unnoticed. Therefore, gender appropriateness may not always be the main criterion to comply with, as other assessment criteria may be more salient and sometimes be in conflict with the doing of gender criterion.

From the researcher's (the critical feminist) perspective gender is viewed only or mainly as negative (assumption 4), but it can also be seen in other ideological lights. Perhaps there are also positive reasons or motives for doing gender. People may try to avoid being seen as doing gender inappropriately and experience it as a risk, a source of compliance or as a source of resistance. Arguably, for many doing gender is viewed as positive, albeit not always and without ambivalence. A counter assumption to the risk assumption would then be that people do gender because it is in line with who they feel they are and how they want to express and reinforce their identity. Perhaps gender is a source of self-esteem and confirmation, driven by positive feelings rather than by anticipation and the fear of a negative judgment from others.

This may sound very conservative and undermine the feminist project (and therefore worthy of rejection on ideological grounds) but it is not necessarily the case. Seeking a positive sense of self can be self-constraining and oppressive, as Foucault and his advocates would argue (Foucault, 1980; Knights and Willmott, 1989). Critical work aiming to achieve resistance, emancipation and change needs to consider this paradoxical element. It would therefore be worthwhile to investigate if and when (and what, why and how questions can be added) people feel positive about doing gender.

Focusing on if and when people feel positive about gender doing means expressing an interest not only in interactions but also in the views of those making up the interactions, what they bring to those interactions and how they assess what is happening. What is displayed of the self and other elements may have very different meanings for people involved in the interactions, both regarding the motives for doing gender and those assessing the doing. Arguably, those at risk of being assessed and those doing the assessment may view one and the same interaction quite differently. However, West and Zimmerman seem to indicate that most of the interactions they have studied are characterized by shared meanings and smoothness around the gender doing. However most of their examples focus one-sidedly on one category in so-called interactions, for example, female athletes or managers exhibiting some sign of femininity or male kindergarten teachers taking care of technical issues and/or doing physical activities with children. Supposedly, those who are assessing these people 'at risk', are also exposed to judgments by the people they assess, that is, the female athletes and the male kindergarten teachers. This invokes the question of for whom is something gender-appropriate? Perhaps there is less of a consensus around this than gender researchers implied.

In short, the alternative assumption ground could be summarized as follows.

1 Gender is not necessarily always an ever-present and quasi-essential feature of interactions but varies from situation to situation, suggesting that the 'when' of gender doing is important to study.
2 In some situations gender is in the forefront of interaction and seen as significant and accountable, but in others gender is optional or at least less or non-significant. Worthy investigations would then be when and how gender is made significant, that is, when and how do people engage in 'gender-appropriate' behavior? And when, if ever, do they not?
3 Doing gender is often not a matter of (successfully) adapting to homogeneous norms, where the doing and assessment align. Instead, gender doing is characterized by diversity and fragmentation – and the presence of norms calling for people not to do gender. Hence, gender doings often involve misalignment, friction and conflict.
4 Doing gender is not (only) driven by the risk of being assessed, that is, negatively motivated, but (also) experienced as a positive value.
5 Gender is not only embedded in interaction but also anchored in gendered identity, forming a strong input to interaction and a key trigger for doing gender outside obvious interaction contexts, that is, people can do gender in order to confirm who they think they are, also outside the presence of an evaluating other.

5. Considering assumptions in relation to the audience

The five assumptions emerging from our critical scrutiny of the focused text can be related to a wide set of audiences within the overall category of feminism and gender studies. Advocates who regard the gender doing perspective as a root metaphor portraying gender as entrapment and as a source of discrimination and repression may feel that the alternative assumptions will jeopardize the entire research program and its purpose. In order to better appeal to their concerns, the framing of the alternative assumptions needs to be supplemented with a stronger critical vocabulary, such as oppression, resistance, gender as a trap and so on, which are easy to connect to the suggested assumptions. In other words, assumption-challenging needs to be balanced with a recognition that one shares the same critical agenda to a high degree.

One could also imagine that some members of the doing gender school would welcome the suggested challenges and the new research questions derived from the problematization. After a large number of studies have drawn on and confirmed West and Zimmerman's gender doing school, there may be a sense of saturation and an interest in considering some new points of departure. The proposed alternatives are broadly in line with many of the school's ideas about level and dynamics and take the interaction idea quite seriously. Indeed, it develops this a bit by bit, for example, pointing at asymmetrical and non-aligned interactions and drawing attention to the diversities of meanings involved.

The experienced novelty of the alternative assumptions may vary quite a lot among gender students, depending on how well they are read in versions of gender studies considering poststructuralism(s). Those who are very familiar with this stream may not be inclined to see the new assumptions as particularly novel or surprising. Our suggestions may be viewed as a moderate move towards taking fragmentation and differentiation seriously. For some, particularly with a more empirical interest and curiosity about empirical variation, the set of ideas/considerations of doing, un-doing (resisting) and non-doing (bypassing) gender as a normative order, may offer a helpful framework for making new and unexpected research questions possible.

6. Evaluating the alternative assumption ground

Before finally formulating (publishing) the alternative assumptions and the research questions that emerge from this, it is important to think carefully about how to craft the text so that it has appeal and is experienced as a dialogue bringing the targeted audience– which can be narrow or broad – together with the author. As Davis (1971) emphasized, a key issue is to try to challenge an audience's taken-for-granted assumptions in such a way that they see the new idea as interesting and are willing to buy the line of argument. This involves confirming parts of their existing assumptions, while problematizing others. One does not of course need to follow this 'success formula' for triggering the 'that's interesting' response from a targeted group. One may also use more confrontational tactics and hope it may lead to a positive response. But here we are mainly considering the ideal of getting an audience to accept an assumption challenge. And even if one goes for a more confrontational assumption-challenging approach, it is always good to consider the potential readers' response to the assumption challenge in a published research text.

As one aim is to communicate with a deeply committed group that regards gender as an oppressive force and sees gender quality as needing to be maintained, it seems important to highlight situations or themes that are high on gender presence and have clear constraining consequences on those forced/encouraged/expected to do gender. Then alternative ones, where gender doing is less clearly present or does not seem to be significant, can be introduced, as can the idea of gender doing as something positive. Likewise, risk can be contrasted with joy as a driver for gender doing. Similarly, gender as a constraining effect can be contrasted with gender as sometimes a positive force. Perhaps doing gender is driven as much by the hope as the risk of being accountable in terms of gender?

Furthermore, West and Zimmerman suggest that we do not 'have the option of being seen by others as female or male' (1987: 130), but we may have the option of emphasizing or not emphasizing this in both our interactions with, and in our assessments of, others. We may not be so risk-averse about how others may assess us and may take some chances in behaving in ways that do not fully conform with the expectation of others. We may, as scrutinizers of others, be tolerant and open to the possibility that people may act in ways that will make it hard to place them in specific gender categories. West and Zimmerman (2009) deny that this means the 'undoing' of gender, and would probably be even more negative towards our suggestion to also assume the possibility and existence of the *non-doing of gender* and open up to studying it. West and Zimmerman (2009) suggest re-doing as a possibility. One could open up towards studying the limits of the gender constraints and the options of doing or re-doing gender. The alternative research question could then be: Are we doomed to do gender? Perhaps we can not only do, re-do, and un-do gender, but also non-do gender?

We see research questions considering the spectrum of options as leading to novel insights: the doing, re-doing, un-doing and non-doing of gender provides alternative vocabularies. One could possibly also add the 'less doing of gender', if (or when) other categories may matter more, but we may give space to the inevitability of gender doing (at least in societies that are available for empirical study). But even when sex categories are used or responded to, it is perhaps worth asking more openly whether this necessarily means 'to affirm different category incumbents "essentially different natures"', as West and Zimmerman (2009: 114) suggest. Perhaps 'sex category essentialism' could be opened up to inquiry rather than being postulated and research questions could be asked that would avoid the pitfall of just confirming the assumption.

These research questions then involve not just asking how people do gender, but also:

- Do people do gender?
- If so, when do they do it?
- When (if ever) is it downplayed or avoided?
- Is gender doing only or mainly driven by an awareness of the risk for accountability or are there other, less negative, gender-doing drivers at stake?

Our task here is not to suggest very specific research questions that can inform specific empirical studies. Instead, our broadly formulated questions illustrate how one can move from a key text (or a school) and its assumptions and, based on that, develop a set of alternative assumptions that forms inputs for new inquiry areas, and examine how these new areas can be boiled down more distinctly, given the specific interests of the researcher and the local conditions for a study.

Conclusion

We have in this chapter illustrated how one can work with the problematization methodology through two examples. In both of these, we targeted some key texts, but as we have emphasized, a broader set of literature can also be chosen for a problematization exercise. Moreover, in order to carry out a successful problematization it is likely to be central to focus on both specific theories as well as have a good grasp of the broader sub-fields to which they belong. It is important to bear in mind that the idea here is not to deliver a foolproof critique of targeted texts or areas, but to read these in order to produce alternative assumptions encouraging different research questions. The alternative assumptions are not necessarily 'better' than those challenged, but after some time the latter may be worn out and parts of a research field may be caught by these and will then mainly conduct predictable research (as a lot of doing gender studies seems to have done during recent times).

There is of course no guarantee that the alternative set of questions constructed from the problematization of Dutton et al.'s and West and Zimmermann's studies will lead to the development of more interesting and influential theories. But given that they deliberately challenge some significant assumptions in the existing literature on organizational identity and gender studies – rather than merely being designed for filling yet another gap – the theories generated by them could potentially be seen as interesting and thus become influential.

7

WHY DOES GAP-SPOTTING DOMINATE WHEN IT REDUCES THE CHANCE TO CREATE INTERESTING THEORIES?

In Chapters 5 and 6, we described and illustrated how the problematization methodology offers a distinct alternative to the dominant mode of using the literature in a field for formulating research questions. However, in order to more fully be able to embrace the problematization methodology as a possible option, it is important to also investigate the social aspects of doing non-conventional research, in particular to what extent such a methodology is supported by the broader research community. It is vital for the individual researcher to learn how to navigate academic fields that sometimes do not welcome ideas that go against conventional wisdom. This includes addressing the researcher's own priorities, objectives and identity projects in the light of community/autonomy tradeoffs. The aim of this chapter is thus to investigate the social, political and identity aspects of assumption-challenging research. We begin by discussing the paradoxical situation of why most researchers seem to use gap-spotting as a way of generating research questions when it is increasingly known that such consensus-confirming research rarely leads to interesting and influential theories. In other words, why do we do so much of this less or non-interesting, perhaps even boring, research?

We identify three important drivers behind this paradoxical situation: institutional conditions; professional norms; and researchers' identity constructions. Thereafter we review and discuss possible ways of revising these drivers so that they more actively support and encourage not only gap-spotting research but also more assumption challenging research, such as that generated by the problematization methodology. We argue in particular for the development and encouragement of a more reflexive and inventive scholarship in the social sciences.

Possible drivers behind the prevalence of gap-spotting research in social science

In Chapters 3 and 4 we showed that there is a near total dominance of using gap-spotting in constructing research questions in the social sciences, leading mostly to the incremental development of existing theories rather than the production of more interesting and influential theories. There are of course studies that do not adapt a gap-spotting logic, but work with a new idea and/or combine critical thinking about the tradition one is drawing upon and some novel input from empirical work or synthesis with some other theory. However, clear deviations from gap-spotting are, according to our review, rare and do not often include ambitious problematization. That incremental consensus-confirming work is much more common than consensus-challenging contributions is unsurprising and not in itself a problem. A central part of research is to build upon earlier work and there is not space here for an enormous amount of assumption-challenging studies. If everybody were to be busy challenging each other's – or their own – assumptions all the time it would not be so good. High-impact studies are by definition very rare.

What is surprising and worrying – at least for the editors and other commentators cited in Chapter 1 – is that the number of consensus-challenging studies is disappointingly low. The strong dominance of incremental gap-spotting research is even more puzzling, as it is well-known that it is consensus-challenging and not consensus-seeking theories that tend to receive most attention and become influential. Moreover, given the availability of ideas and perspectives that emphasize problematization in research, it is remarkable that the majority of researchers, from positivists to postmodernists, seem to use gap-spotting, rather than problematization, as their preferred – or at least practically used – way of constructing research questions and, consequently, as the major rationale for their studies.

An interesting (research) question is thus: *Why does gap-spotting continue to be the dominant way of constructing research questions from existing literature, as expressed in research texts?*[1] This question is important from a more general sociological point, as a way to create a general understanding of how contemporary research functions. It is also of importance in terms of policy implications for government, university administration, research councils and other decision makers. But in this book, addressing primarily the research practitioner, understanding the forces and mechanisms in operation leading to a disinclination to do novel and interesting research is especially vital in order to avoid unreflectively falling into mainstream work orientations. We want instead to support the struggle for more autonomy, deviation, imagination and carefully grounded choices in academic work. In order to deviate from a strong, but in some key respects problematic, mainstream, one needs to understand the mechanisms and reproductive

---

[1] This research question is to a degree based on problematization. We question the assumption of the natural or rational character of doing gap-spotting research. We say 'to a degree' as we have worked with reflexive and critical approaches to research methodology for some time (Alvesson and Sköldberg, 2009; Sandberg and Tsoukas, 2011) and also heavily draw upon Davis (1971), whose ideas we do not seriously investigate and scrutinize. There is thus a strong element of pre-programmed problematization in our text as well, that is, one following and reproducing a skeptical line of inquiry as well as Davis's view.

powers behind the latter. Here the researcher needs to consider the broader socio-political situation and place methodological preferences and habits in their larger context.

Earlier in Chapter 4 we rejected the idea that active problematization has been used in some studies but disguised in the actual research text. If problematization is hidden or downplayed in research texts, a question emerges: why do researchers refrain from formulating their work in ways that, according to studies of interesting theories, may increase the interest in and the influence of their work? This is puzzling because as Mizruchi and Fein noted, whatever 'motivates the effort of the scientist, most people hope that their work will be, if not revolutionary, at least influential' (1999: 653). In other words, why would anyone bother to assert a knowledge claim that is less likely to generate interest and attention from the field? And as we have seen, gap-spotting is not just a characteristic of 'conventional' research but also of more 'progressive' versions inspired by poststructuralism.

The question is particularly interesting as it could be argued that scholars seem to 'voluntarily' refrain from addressing existing studies in a way that, according to Davis (1971) and others, would increase the likelihood of producing an interesting and influential theory. Could it be a way in which our institutions – universities, research communities and journals - strongly encourage or 'force' researchers into gap-spotting research? Immediately one could perhaps see this as absurd. Is not the main ambition of institutions and researchers to develop novel and influential knowledge? Surely, all participants in the research community, such as university and schools, departments, management and journal editors, are strongly supportive of any realistic and ambitious effort to develop ground-breaking research – or are they?

The answer to the question of why there are so few examples of problematization is not likely to lie inside the research texts investigated in Chapters 3 and 4. Although they indicate that gap-spotting is the favored approach – or a possible rhetoric legitimating research papers – they do not really tell us why researchers use gap-spotting as the preferred or at least their chosen way of constructing research questions. Instead, the answer is more likely to be found in the *scientific field* within which these texts are located and produced. Research texts are crafted in a socio-political context and the need to adapt to the rules of the field is strong (Alvesson et al., 2008; Hassard and Keleman, 2002). Scientific fields consist of a range of social norms and methodological rules that guide and regulate the production and publication of scientific knowledge in significant ways (Bourdieu, 2004; Cole and Cole, 1967; Kuhn, 1970).

Important questions might include the following. What kind of possibilities or constraints characterizes a scientific field? What social norms regulate the production of scientific knowledge and publication of scientific texts within a particular scientific field? What are the expectations and constraints expressed by editors and reviewers as representatives of the research community exercising control over texts? What kinds of reward system (promotion, funding, recognition, and so on) exist within the field and how do they regulate the conduct of producing research, especially the production of research reports?

Although many of these norms are part of the taken-for-granted landscape of the scientific field and therefore hard to detect (Gadamer, 1994; Gouldner, 1970), we think that the viewpoints below are important to consider for understanding the (over-) emphasis on gap-spotting and the shortage of assumption-challenging studies. More specifically, we think there are three broad and interacting drivers, offering explanations for this paradoxical behavior among researchers in the social sciences: institutional conditions, professional norms within the academic field and researchers' identity constructions.

Institutional conditions

Institutional conditions refer to how institutions (governments, universities, schools and departments, funding bodies and so on) and their policies regulate the conduct of research, especially the production of research reports. An overarching institutional condition that seems to encourage incremental gap-spotting research is the current practice of using *designated journal lists* for evaluating academic research performance.

Universities and researchers in many countries across the globe are increasingly governed by various assessment formulas introduced by governments for evaluating academic research performance, such as the RAE/REF in the UK and ERA in Australia (Bessant et al., 2003; Leung, 2007; Willmott, 1995, 2011). A key performance indicator in those assessment formulas is the number of articles published in highly ranking journals within a designated journal list. This has meant that practically the only research performance that counts in many elite (and elite-wannabee) schools and universities today is publications in A-listed journals.

As noted by many across the entire scientific field(s) as a whole (Adler and Harzing, 2009; Lawrence, 2008), the use of such journal lists is likely to encourage researchers to concentrate on publishing articles in particular journals rather than trying to develop more original knowledge by identifying and challenging the assumptions underlying existing literature. In management studies, Macdonald and Kam observed that: 'All but forgotten in the desperation to win the game is publication as a means of communicating research findings for the public benefit' (2007: 702). And in science Lawrence noted that the use of journal lists for evaluating academic research performance has meant that 'scientists have been forced to downgrade their primary aim of making discoveries to publishing as many papers as possible' (2008: 1).

The pressure to publish in highly ranked journals does not necessarily in itself reduce innovative work, and in some ways it promotes it, but as we will discuss below, these journals tend to emphasize incremental gap-spotting research more than innovation and intellectual boldness, at least this seem to be what they publish

(Bouchikhi and Kimberly, 2001; de Rond and Miller, 2005; Pfeffer, 2007; Starbuck, 2006, 2009). They tend to be cautious and conservative, using established researchers as reviewers.

Professional norms within the academic field

Journals, editors and reviewers are the main professional norm setters for how research is conducted and what research is published (Baruch et al., 2008) within the academic field. Incremental gap-spotting research is strongly encouraged by the 'adding-to-the literature' norm within many leading journals (e.g., Johanson, 2007; Pratt, 2009) as the primary evidence for research contribution. For example, based on her 26 years as the top journal *Administrative Science Quarterly*'s managing editor and her reading of more than 19,000 reviews and more than 8,000 decision letters, Johanson firmly advises authors to adhere to the adding-to-the literature norm because 'if you can't make a convincing argument that you are filling an important gap in the literature, you will have a hard time establishing that you have a contribution to make to that literature' (2007: 292). The prevalence of the adding-to-the-literature norm for contribution is also evident in Miller et al.'s observation that top-tier journals increasingly force researchers into incremental gap-spotting research by encouraging work 'on topics that fit neatly within today's popular theories and allow the development and tweaking of those theories' (2009: 278).

The strong adding-to-the-literature norm in leading journals does not necessarily mean that challenging dominant assumptions is excluded or directly discouraged. However, its emphasis on carefully relating one's own study to the existing literature tends to encourage researchers to find gaps and not to move that far away from the established body of work in their specific sub-field.

The demand to meticulously relate one's study to the existing literature is also underpinned by a specific kind of *rigor* that is upheld within many journals. It typically means (1) a requirement of a systematic and overly pedantic vacuum cleaning of existing literature, as a way to show how one's own study contributes to existing literature and (2) an emphasis on carrying out empirical research through detailed codification procedures or statistical treatment without asking questions about there being something more fundamentally problematic with the existing literature or whether the data really are valuable indicators of the phenomena supposedly addressed. As the outgoing editors of *Journal of Management Studies* observed in their final editorial note: 'The emphasis on improving the rigor of theorizing and of empirical method ... may have led to more incremental research questions being addressed' (Clark and Wright, 2009: 6).

Incremental gap-spotting research is further driven by the increasing tendency among academics to *pigeonhole* themselves (and their subject matters) into narrow and well-mastered areas. Such pigeonholing helps to boost their productivity and to meet academic performance criteria in the sense that: one knows the literature, goes to the right conferences, cultivates a network of people that matter, is familiar with the norms and rules of the journals in the sub-area, and is therefore capable of successfully publishing incremental contributions regularly. But the likelihood of generating frame-bending and high-impact research through such pigeonholing is typically low. In particular, there are often (1) strong expectations (among reviewers and editors) that people working within a specific sub-field will cite a significant part of all the work within it and (2) limited space, energy and tolerance for bringing in literature from outside the sub-field, as a way to open up new areas of inquiry (Bourdieu, 2004; Pierson, 2007; Starbuck, 2003). Sometimes this pigeonhole thinking comes through very strongly. One of us received the following reason from a reviewer for why his paper should be rejected: 'I'm just not convinced that this paper works as a piece of leadership research that can be satisfactorily situated within existing approaches and debates.' But perhaps innovative research does not easily situate itself within the existing literature in a specific sub-field and instead breaks out and challenges it.

Gap-spotting research is also promoted by the strongly held *accumulation* norm in social science that knowledge is supposed to advance through incremental accumulation within a particular field. Using the organization studies field as an illustration, as Litchfield and Thomson, the founders of *Administrative Science Quarterly*, lay out in their vision of the field of organization studies: 'scholars should build a cumulative, comprehensive, general body of theory about administration' (Palmer, 2006: 537). This accumulation norm continues to dominate. For example, in its criteria for publication, the *Academy of Management Journal* stipulates that 'submissions should clearly communicate the nature of their theoretical contribution in relation to the existing management and organizational literatures'. Similarly, the *Journal of Management Studies* says that its main criterion for publication is that a submitted paper should contribute 'significantly to the development of coherent bodies of knowledge'.

The accumulation norm tends to reinforce the gap-spotting logic by requiring researchers to adopt a systematic, analytical and often narrow focus, which makes them unable to ask more fundamental and skeptical questions that may encourage some significant rethinking of the subject matter in question. The accumulation norm also gives an impression of a collective project signaling reason, rationality and progress and may work as an antidote to a lurking feeling that social research has strong elements of subjectivity, arbitrariness and relativism (Pfeffer, 1993). To convince ourselves that we are not fluffy and unreliable but really rational and scientific, it makes sense to engage in traditional and seemingly robust logics, such as firmly building on and incrementally adding to, established bodies of knowledge. Hence, gap-spotting research may be used to legitimate not only a specific piece of research but also the scientific project itself and, thus, will preserve and reproduce knowledge accumulation as a fundamental scientific ideal, despite this being untenable as shown by Kuhn (1970) and scholars emphasizing the multi-paradigmatic and contested nature of social science (Burrell and Morgan, 1979; Delanty, 2005). A note of caution is important here, as the accumulation norm in other disciplines within the social sciences may not be as prevalent as in the management and organization studies field.

Closely related to the accumulation ideal is the *crediting* norm, which stresses the need to build on and acknowledge the work of other scholars. Although citation is vital in research publications, there seems to be an increasingly strong expectation to vacuum-clean a narrow field and cite almost everything within it, even if it makes the text more disrupted and harder to read and the references do not add anything. As Gabriel observed:

> Publishing is now a long process, involving numerous revisions, citing authors one does not care for, engaging with arguments one is not interested in and seeking to satisfy different harsh masters, often with conflicting or incompatible demands, while staying within a strict word limit. Most authors will go through these tribulations and the drudgery of copious revisions, accepting virtually any criticism and any recommendation with scarcely any complaint, all in the interest of getting published. (2010: 764)

It is also a strong requirement from journals to cite work that has been published by them as a way to increase their impact factor and ultimately to get published. For example, both authors, who recently published articles in a top-tier journal, discovered in the proofs that the journal editors had inserted references from their own journal without permission from the authors. While this kind of 'coercive citation' is occurring across the board it is considerably more common in management journals (Wilhite and Fong, 2012: 543).

Journals function as a strong disciplinary regime (Foucault, 1980), including both careful surveillance of exactly what authors do (in terms of result deliveries) and normalization through pointing at any deviation from what is the norm for writing and publishing. As such it is a mixed blessing, constraining and productive at the same time. On the whole, the quality-reinforcing elements are the most prominent and journals also encourage and demand a degree of innovation and novelty. Clearly, papers benefit from many reviews and revisions over time, but the increasingly detailed expectation that authors must comply almost fully with the demands of reviewers and make all concerned more or less satisfied is sometimes counterproductive, in particular given the research ideals we advocate in this book.

To develop original ideas and engage in independent thinking is counteracted by a demand to ground everything that is being said in 'existing literature' in a specific sub-field. In principle, it is possible to do both. But time, effort, intellectual focus and text space typically mean that there is a conflict between the norms that demand everything should be tightly connected to literature, data and methodological rules, on the one hand, and more imaginative and innovative research efforts, on the other. More imaginative efforts often call for a less detailed focus on what exists and more discretion. In particular, the current focus in many review processes on fault-finding and compliance with reviewers' and editors' comments with the aim of making the submitted paper more tightly related to existing literature is likely to produce incremental research rather than encourage the development of novel and challenging ideas (Bedeian, 2003, 2004; Tsang and Frey, 2007). The strict exercising of disciplinary power does not facilitate creative and challenging work and knowledge contributions.

Researchers' identity construction

The above institutional conditions and professional norms exercise a strong normative control over the way research is conducted and reported in research texts. Through a long and extended socialization into the academic field, most researchers internalize those norms and conditions and develop what can be called a *gap-spotting habitus* (to partly borrow a term from Bourdieu). By following this habitus, we reproduce its dominance and force others to comply; giving gap-spotting the status of the proper or 'right' way of generating research questions and developing theories within social studies. In other words, we become gap-spotters doing incremental gap-spotting research.

This gap-spotting identity is further reinforced by the fact that many researchers within the social sciences take very seriously the demand to publish regularly in the 'right' journals. At least this is what is expressed at conferences and other social interactions among researchers. People report that they feel the pressure to publish, otherwise the school may fall back a step or so in the rankings, they may not get tenure, or their promotion may not be as rapid as it would be otherwise. For many, a strong responsiveness to expectations has become natural and self-evident. Academics in many disciplines are turning themselves into gap-spotting sub-specialists eager to pump out as many journal articles as possible rather than becoming more genuine scholars, wanting to do really novel, challenging and significant research. Identity constructions seem to be more about how much is being published and where rather than about original knowledge and unique contributions. The question 'Who am I?' is increasingly answered with 'I am a person who has published in this or that journal.' We see indications of this identity construction all the time in author presentations in journals. Here, many people mention an affiliation and then emphasize where they have published. As identity markers publication outlets are apparently central. A particularly problematic effect of constructing an identity based on where you publish is that it can easily lead to what Willmott (2011) labeled 'journal fetishism', that is, researchers will start to care more about the publication outlet than the actual research contribution.

This somewhat perverse and excessive focus on journal publication as identity marker and career booster further drives researchers to embrace incremental gap-spotting research and simultaneously downplays more genuine scholarly research – where extensive reading coupled with a familiarity with, and interest in, a wide set of ideas are important. As Barnett (2010) poignantly observed, if a colleague peeks into your office and sees you are reading a book you almost feel embarrassed and guilty; you are supposed to write papers not read books. Similarly, Gabriel observed that the majority of his colleagues 'read mostly the abstracts and spend relatively little time carefully assimilating detailed arguments, which suggests to me that, for many reading (with the notable exception of reading for the purpose of writing a peer review) has become a less important activity than writing' (2010: 762). This leads to the possibility of academics writing for fellow writers, who are only interested in 'casting their eyes on whatever promotes their own writing agendas' (2010: 762).

It is important not to exaggerate here. The observations mentioned are mainly from business schools and they are not necessarily representative of what goes on within other disciplines within the social sciences. Far from all academic fields and individuals go this far in narrow instrumentalism. One should not exaggerate critique either. Publications in the right journals are not contradictory to broader scholarship and a strong intellectual interest, including curiosity, openness and a willingness to take some risks and try to be imaginative and creative. Journals do demand a contribution and the highly ranked journals can often demand at least a degree of creativity and novelty for accepting and publishing a paper. But far from all work characterized by the latter is readily compatible with contemporary journal publications and, in particular, not with the requirement to constantly publish papers for prestigious journals. Many intellectual projects require something broader that does not easily fit into the standard journal format. Hence, even if our picture of instrumental and opportunistic researchers domesticated and rewarded by journals allowing mainly narrow, incremental and boring papers may not apply to certain fields and areas within the social sciences, there are many worrying signs and examples worthy of taking seriously.

The problem is twofold in that (1) the contemporary journal format is the optimum for all kinds of research and scholarly orientations and (2) contemporary professional norms are giving too much priority to incremental gap-spotting research, which taken together foster a journal publication technician rather than a 'genuine' scholar. In particular, incremental gap-spotting research with its typically narrow and instrumental approach contradicts problematization and assumption-challenging and, thus, makes the generation of more novel and influential work near impossible. The gap-spotting mode is further reinforced when social researchers together – in reviews, in promotion committees, in career advising, in pub and conference talk – do identity regulation of others and themselves (Alvesson and Willmott, 2002), naturalizing and normalizing publications in 'top journals' (only). A too strong focus on journal outlets partly goes in a direction that undermines the chances of more interesting work is getting produced. We, as a research community, apparently foster a gap-spotting mode – not a scholarship mode – as the key ingredient in researchers' identity construction. Researchers eager and capable enough to use a broad set of intellectual resources and be imaginative and challenging are a rarity – at least when it comes to appearing in leading journals.

The relationship among professional norms, institutional conditions and researchers' identity construction

The victim-of-the-system explanation

It is possible to see the interplay between institutional conditions, professional norms and researchers' identity construction as a tight system from which is highly difficult to break away. One line of argumentation would thus be to emphasize the connections and mutually reinforcing effects of the three key drivers behind the prevalence of incremental gap-spotting research. Institutions emphasize rankings, journals and academics eager to be successful (or otherwise facing the material and symbolic consequences) and strive for ranking improvements, and identity projects are caught up in the rankings and differentiations: to be a good academic means to publish in A-listed journals, and you must do whatever it takes to get published in those journals. As those who publish in A-listed journals are typically viewed as 'better' academics, others follow and imitate. Deviations and failures mean material and symbolic losses: employment, career, status and self-esteem may be at risk.

For most people, such a tightly regulated system makes it almost impossible to spend several years writing a really innovative book (or even a set of papers). Innovative and influential writings like those that emerged a couple of decades ago are rarely seen nowadays. In our own field, organization studies, we rarely see any books published that are of the same magnitude and significance as some of the widely read and respected research monographs of the 1970s, 1980s and early 1990s, despite there being many more active researchers today than 20–40 years ago.

Instead, academics in most fields are furiously trying to publish in A-listed journals, whose grip over a researcher's time, focus and self is being reinforced. As many universities and schools, especially internationally leading ones, are rewarding success in terms of the number of publications in A-listed journals, performing less well on this one-dimensional scale means researchers are jeopardizing their academic career possibilities and perhaps their egos. Many researchers struggle to gain even a modest level of success, and in some places, performance monitoring and resource allocation simply mean that without a steady flow of journal publications there may be consequences, such as teaching load increases, money for conferences and books drying up, and it will be difficult to find sufficient time and support to do ambitious research. Colleagues may also feel that you let them down, as the absence of sufficient number of journal articles may jeopardize the institution's place in the rankings. In order to survive in such a tightly regulated system a researcher is more or less forced into incremental gap-spotting research in a highly specialized area.

While the 'victim of the system' explanation for the shortage of interesting and influential theories in social studies intuitively makes sense, it is a partial explanation and in many places the system is neither so tight nor so constraining. It is perhaps surprising how few protests there have been about this 'evil' system, despite frequent complaints in conversations among people. (It is difficult to marshal an effective protest against these kinds of regimes, partly because it is not easy to suggest alternatives, partly because those not complying may face consequences: see Sauder and Espeland, 2009). The situation seems to persist, even if it seems undesirable, partly because of the more or less voluntary reproduction of it by those caught up in it and also because it has many winners who are reluctant to change it. As Starbuck noted, when such a perverse situation persists, it is almost always when 'someone is benefiting from the situation. So who are the major beneficiaries of non-progress in the development of knowledge?' (2006: 94).

Most researchers and institutions on the successful end of the scale can be seen as benefiting from this perverse situation. It provides university top management and deans with a powerful tool to control and monitor the research performance of faculty. Top-tier journals receive increased submissions and status through achieving high impact factors. The careers of some successful researchers are boosted as well as their power positions within the academic community. PhD students get clear rules for how to operate their careers and may feel their anxiety reduce, at least until they get the reviews for their submissions. At the same time, in particular for deans of less successful schools, publication regimes tend to underscore low status and it is difficult to fully direct energy to other worthwhile tasks, such as research supporting local community or social policies, as this seldom leads to publications in top-tier journals or books with leading publishers. Deans with successful researchers may also find management difficult, as the 'star' researchers' track record provide them with a strong power base.

The being in-the-charge-of-the-system explanation

Above, we made a case for how the three elements (institutional conditions, professional norms and researchers' identity construction) can be seen as a tightly coupled system forcing social researchers (as victims or beneficiaries) into incremental gap-spotting research. But one can also argue for a less deterministic view and much looser connection between the three elements. Governments and university administrations are not in themselves particularly preoccupied with specific forms of research. They would probably applaud the signs of great innovations and high-impact research. However, they are primarily concerned with getting value for money, help in resource allocation and creating an impression of rational control over the spending of taxpayers' money.

All these concerns are of course legitimate. Resources are not endless and it is important not to spread these thinly over everyone, irrespective of research capacity and productivity. Accountability is important for academics also and it needs to be acknowledged that not everyone doing research is capable of producing valuable knowledge. With the significant expansion of higher education during recent decades and the increased focus on research output, the ratio between people trying to produce research and people interested in reading and learning from their efforts becomes increasingly unfavorable, from a knowledge producer's/author's point of view.

If professional groups decided to upgrade assumption-challenging studies and downplay consensus-seeking adding-to-the-literature studies, this would not go against regulatory bodies' need for finding ways of spending resources in a reasonable way and getting some indicators of how various universities, schools and research groups are performing. In the UK, for example, the research assessment review committees are made up of academics, who have significant discretion in evaluating institutions. Similarly, journal editors have extensive discretion about which publication policies the particular journal should embrace. They could therefore make policies that encourage imaginative studies rather than merely incremental gap-spotting research.

It is perhaps even more important to point out that most researchers have considerable discretion when it comes to how they can shape their career. For example, not all people strive to get tenure at a very prestigious university, and even those who do, are only strongly subordinated to do 'whatever it takes' for a short period before they get tenure (or move to another place). Research-active academics are tenured during most of their working life, and many will have more or less guaranteed time for research in their contracts. (Even if the tenure system is weakened, most [tenured] academics have fairly safe jobs, and qualified senior academics even more so. In many countries employment security at universities is still extremely good.) Some researchers are also sufficiently diligent and gifted enough that they can, without too much effort, reach the minimum number of publications required, thus being able to spend extensive time on more innovative projects. So the complaint one sometimes hears that 'I need to publish in certain types of journals in certain types of ways, otherwise I have to teach more, will not get my pay increase, the dean will look negatively at me, my promotion may be delayed …' is not entirely convincing.

One could actually reverse the top-down logic and argue that it is *not* institutional arrangements – rankings, funding, performance pressure from the top – that drive the process downwards, but that it works the opposite way. It is (we) academics – through their choices and priorities – who establish and revise norms and form journals (as authors, reviewers, editors, members of associations running the journals) that probably have the strongest impact on how universities and professional institutions actually do their assessments. Researchers as individuals and collectives are in significant ways in charge of how research should be conducted and decide what research counts as good and should be published. The major problem is hardly that, as one often hears, writers are good and evaluators are not: (we) writers are as bad as (we) editors and reviewers – they (we) are the same persons (although the double-blind reviewer position may sometimes bring out the worst in people [us], as Gabriel, 2010, remarks).

We are exercising concertive control over ourselves, voluntarily building our own constraining (and seductive) rules and norms, and willingly giving up a lot of possible discretion (Barker, 1993). After all, who is producing the research texts, who is giving the feedback and the recommendations and decisions for which papers and books should be published and how the research texts should look like? We all do. As researchers we decide about our own journals – our acts decide rankings and so on. Collectively, academics control the norms for good research and, thus, indirectly, to a considerable degree form, bend and translate how governments' and other institutions' policies influence the research practice.

There are of course limits to our discretion as individuals and there is a complicated structure-agency set of relations involved. Institutionalized arrangements have strong reproductive tendencies and the established rules of the game are not always so easy to change from below. Similarly, centralized moves, such as a highly differentiated research funding based on quantitative output performance, sometimes have drastic effects (Adler and Harzing, 2009). But institutional policies in themselves do not mean the discrimination of imaginative, consensus-challenging work as long as this is carried out productively. Nor is consensus-challenging work necessarily more time-consuming to carry out than consensus-confirming, incremental, gap-spotting studies. But it is difficult to come up with and develop good ideas if there is a strong focus on getting all the technicalities right, associated with a gap-spotting rigor. It is difficult to fully master a narrow sub-speciality *and* read broadly and variedly in order to get new ideas and break out from the sub-speciality box.

What the 'being-in-charge-of-the-system' explanation suggests is that – if only researchers want and dare – there are ample of opportunities to put social studies back on track again. Below we point to how specific changes in institutional arrangements around governance of research, professional norms, and researcher identities can reduce the serious shortage of interesting and influential studies.

Putting social science back on track: ways of encouraging innovative and influential research

The near omnipresent requirement to continuously publish in 'high-quality' journals has meant that most social scientists have lost sight of, or have strongly downplayed, the most overriding goal and ultimate purpose of social studies, namely, to create and produce original knowledge that matters to organizations and society. In other words, it is not paper production per se that is most important but the creation and production of knowledge that is important and influential. Journal publication is a *means* for facilitating the development, quality assurance and communication of new knowledge, not an end in itself. It can be an excellent means with many advantages, but as emphasized here, there are currently significant problems with the system. Therefore, the most important issue for getting social research back on track is to move away from the current focus on paper production to the production of more innovative and influential ideas and theories that can make a significant difference to both theory and social practice. Encouraging such work requires a substantial rethinking and reworking of institutional conditions, professional norms, researchers identity construction and methodologies for theory development.

Revising institutional conditions

Governments

The primary way in which governments influence research is through their specific research assessment reviews focusing on the number of publications in A-listed journals during a specific period of time. However, using such assessment formula, as the chief indicator for academic research performance and quality is marred by difficulties, in particular, as it tends to encourage incremental gap-spotting research. There is also typically a weak relationship between influential studies in the sense of citation impact and where they are published (Adler and Harzing, 2009; Glick et al., 2007; Singh et al., 2007). As Pfeffer noted, the research on citation counts 'illustrates that a shockingly high proportion of papers, even those published in elite journals, garner *zero* citations, with an even larger percentage obtaining very few' (2007: 1342). However, governments can rectify most of the above problems (and better support a scholarship research mode) by changing and broadening the criteria for assessing academic research performance. One of the most important changes would be to put a significantly higher emphasis on *citation count* as an indicator of research performance. This would stimulate stronger efforts to produce more innovative and influential studies, even if productivity would suffer.

Using the citation count as a performance indicator has of course its own problems, as citations often are skewed in various ways. Method and review papers are, for example, much more frequently cited than empirical studies. There are self-citations, clubs of authors citing each other, texts that are heavily cited because they are often targeted for critique, texts that are very timely, and theories that are simple and therefore easy to remember and, perhaps because of the opportunism of the author and so on. In other words, 'we cite for utility – affirmation, signal, salience, substantiation, and consecration – as much if not more than for quality and intellectual debt' (Baum, 2012: 5). But even though there are complications and uncertainties, citations still say a lot about what is considered to be interesting and significant. Citation scores, however, need to be used cautiously and with critical judgment rather than mechanically. They typically need to be supplemented by peer reviews assessing whether the citation numbers reflect quality and influence.

Another important step that governments can take to encourage more innovative and influential work is to *broaden the publication outlets*. Instead of primarily relying upon a designated journal list other outlets can also be included, such as books, book chapters and practitioner oriented journals and magazines. This would take away the emphasis on (only) publishing frequently in prestigious journals and allow for less narrow and standardized work.

Revising university and departmental policies

The above mentioned ideas could also influence what is being done within universities and departments. For example, hiring, tenure and promotion committees could put a stronger emphasis on citation impact, and on research that has been published not only in a designated journal list but also in other outlets, such as books and book chapters.

One can also reconsider the often *too narrow time frames* in which academics are expected to publish a certain amount of articles. As many have pointed out, such productivity measures tend to encourage incremental research. For example, McMullen and Shepard (2006) showed in their study that a strong pressure to publish a certain number of articles within a short timeframe coupled with a risk of getting punished (increased teaching load and so on) if publication targets are not met, significantly discouraged not only junior but also more senior academics from engaging in more consensus-challenging research.

Another policy change that may encourage the development of more innovative and influential research is to counter narrow instrumentalism. This can be done in several different ways, such as institutionalizing less rapid promotion and reducing extrinsic rewards by counteracting title inflation. For example, one way to counteract title inflation could be to reserve the position of full professor for those that have made significant contributions, rather than emphasizing the quantity of publications. Additional ways to counter narrow instrumentalism could be to remove or reduce payment by journal publication, and using broader research criteria for employment, tenure and promotion, including demands for variation in research topics and methods plus variation in publication outlets.

Schools, departments and scholarly associations could also reduce the dominance of incremental gap-spotting research by nurturing a more reflexive and inventive scholarly orientation and consensus-challenging research through *training and workshops* focusing on these virtues. For example, instead of mainly cultivating academics as paper authors for journals, more training and workshops on questioning assumptions, creative writing, writing for a broader audience and the encouragement of research book publications are needed. Needless to say, we are not arguing against journal publication – it is a key quality improvement and assurance resource tool and major outlet for research – rather, we would argue for opportunities to vary intellectual work and give space to contributions that are less easy to shoehorn into the journal standard format.

Rethinking professional norms

Except for the institutional arrangements instigated by governments, universities and departments, there is a need to rethink professional norms, in particular in relation to journal publication. As outlined above, a highly peculiar norm that has spread rapidly is that authors should comply with almost all of the reviewers' requests, even if, as it happens many times, that the comments from one reviewer are highly inconsistent with the comments from another reviewer. We think the norm requiring such a rigid adoption of reviewers' comments needs to be de-emphasized. Furthermore, most submissions need to be rejected – and we often think that too much is published, even in A-listed journals. But one could imagine journals *upgrading innovative and original ideas* (a consequence would be rejecting many more papers than happens now using that criterion) and then letting authors treat reviewers' comments as collegial advice for how the paper can be improved rather than strict instructions for what to do.

In many or most cases, there is of course a shortage of papers with really good ideas. Therefore, given the space to fill, the use of list-like sets of criteria for what is acceptable (clearly written, sufficient gap-spotting, extensive literature review, conservative anchoring in an established method, and a lengthy method section indicating rationality and rigor, a lot of data summarized, a modest contribution and a call for more research) may be the only option than seems possible for journal editors. And one that is sufficient for getting acceptable papers with incremental contributions. However, if one is interested in more imaginative and novel studies, perhaps using checklists for fault-finding should be de-emphasized.

Another criterion for evaluating submitted papers that needs to be reconsidered is the conventional notion of *rigor*, requesting researchers to systematically vacuum clean existing literature to demonstrate how their own study makes a contribution to that literature. This kind of rigor is often used as the prime mechanism for rejecting a paper in the review process, and often justifiably so, but it may work against really innovative and interesting ideas. In particular, while this kind of rigor is important in incremental gap-spotting research, an alternative form of 'rigor' (quality criteria) could be to emphasize the need to identify and challenge assumptions. In other words, as part of the standard journal policy, it can be requested that authors need to consider carefully the assumptions underlying the existing literature, and how those assumptions shape the understanding and conceptualization of the subject matter in question, thus demonstrating reflexivity as a key quality of 'rigor' (Alvesson and Sköldberg, 2009). In a similar vein, Yanchar et al. argued that researchers engaged in this kind of questioning and critical thinking 'would seek to understand as thoroughly as possible the assumptions that inform their theories and methods and, moreover, those that inform alternatives' (2008: 270). Returning to Foucault again, as a problematizer, our 'role is to raise questions in an effective, genuine way, and to raise them with the greatest possible rigor, with the maximum complexity and difficulty' (Koopman, 2011: 10).

Cultivating a more scholarly identity: from gap-spotter to reflexive inventor

Although changes in government, university and journal policies, such as those discussed above, are important for reducing the shortage of high-impact research, they are only partly helpful because, at the end of the day, it is we academics who decide what we do and how we do it. The impression from the studies and comments discussed previously is that gap-spotting researchers – at least those who make it into to highly ranked journals and therefore 'count' – are not just intelligent, rigorous, diligent, methodologically and theoretically well trained, but also cautious, instrumental, disciplined, career-minded, pedantic and strongly specialized. This gap-spotting identity is, to a degree, difficult to avoid and, as we have emphasized, far from entirely negative. But against this, one could put forward more genuine scholarly values and qualities like being intellectually broad-minded, independent, imaginative, willing to take risks, enthusiastic about intellectual adventures and frequently provocative. This would imply giving priority to discretion and integrity and doing meaningful research that matters rather than prioritizing tenure at a top university, rapid promotion and publishing in the most prestigious journals.

This is also something advocated by Rynes in her concluding note from an *AMJ* editorial forum 'on looking back and looking forward on management research', where she argued that researchers should have a 'higher purpose beyond simply getting another "hit" in a top-tier journal' (2007: 1382). Instead, researchers should be 'committed to ... ideas we care about rather than focusing on what our publications will do for our image, our compensation, or our careers' (2007: 1382). That is, we need less instrumental gap-spotting and publication-prioritizing sub-specialists working for an extended period within one area only and more researchers with a broader outlook, curious, reflective, willing and also able to question their own frameworks and consider alternative positions, and also eager to produce new insights at the risk of some short-term instrumental sacrifices, that is, a more reflexive and inventive scholarship mode. Such 'scholarly research reflects our pressing and irreversible need as human beings to confront the unknown and seek understanding for its own sake. It is tied inextricably to the freedom to think freshly, to see propositions of every kind in an every changing light. And it celebrates the special exhilaration that comes from a new idea' (Boyer, 1990: 17).

In order to win back and cultivate a more reflexive and inventive scholarship among researchers, cultural and identity issues need to be directly targeted. Even if journals should adopt and try to implement an upgrading of interesting work at the expense of technical excellence, the success of this is almost entirely dependent on sufficient numbers of good researchers defining themselves and their work in a more scholarly fashion. This is a task for all of us in academia. It is partly a matter of, on a daily basis, cultivating a specific self-understanding – carried out through research choices, reflexive exercises, thoughtful (and not mainly gap-spotting instrumental) use of networks, collaborations and so on, and partly – in our capacity as research leaders, PhD advisors, colleagues and so on – about influencing others.

There is of course an endless number of ways of doing so. We will only give one example here. In terms of seminar presentations, why only invite people to give a paper? Perhaps visitors could be asked to present and discuss a very interesting book or an article they have been inspired by lately, informing their own research or general line of thinking. As Gabriel (2010) notes, reading and discussing texts is increasingly marginalized – and a continued de-focusing on books can be seen as deeply problematic, calling for countermeasures.

Table 7.1 *The main features of a gap-spotting versus a reflexive and inventive scholarship mode*

Basic features	Gap-spotting mode	Reflexive and inventive scholarship mode
Main focus in theory development	Consensus-seeking: theory development through incremental additions to existing literature, and ignorant about own assumptions and prejudices	Consensus-challenging: theory development by challenging the assumptions underlying existing literature, and a strong awareness of own prejudices
Scope	Researchers often pigeonhole themselves (and subject matters) into a narrowly confined and well-mastered area	Researchers often span across areas and theoretical frameworks in their search for new insights
Research outcome	Additive and incremental theories – often dull and formulaic	Frame-bending theories – often seen as interesting and influential, sometimes controversial
Publication outlets	Journals in designated journal lists	Journals, books, book chapters, articles written for a broader audience

Conclusion

The aim of this chapter was to investigate why gap-spotting continues to be the dominant way of constructing research questions from the existing literature and, based on that, to try to encourage more thoughtful responses from both policymakers at different levels and from researchers individually as well as collectively. In particular, we argued that in order to be able to break away from the dominance of incremental gap-spotting research it is important to become aware of what drives most researchers to adhere to the gap-spotting logic, despite it becoming increasingly known that it is consensus-challenging, not consensus-seeking theories that tend to receive most attention and become influential. We identified three interplaying key drivers behind this puzzling behavior, namely, how specific institutional policies, professional norms and researchers' identity constructions interplay in a way that strongly encourages researchers into gap-spotting research.

As a way forward, we proposed and discussed how specific changes in those key drivers can facilitate the development of more innovative and influential theories. While the 'evil' system of institutional policies for academic ranking, professional norms and researchers' identity constructions appears to be near impossible to break away from, we proposed that researchers may not be as much victims of the system as it looks like. This is because it is we, ourselves, who to a large extent are the developers and executers of the 'evil' system that 'forces' us into incremental gap-spotting research, leading to a shortage of interesting and influential theories. To blame 'the system' for doing incremental, uninteresting research is hardly credible or constructive. As summarized in Table 7.1, we suggested several ways for moving away from a one-sided cultivation of the gap-spotting mode to more actively encouraging a genuine scholarship mode where consensus-challenging rather than consensus-seeking studies are emphasized.

In enabling such a shift, governments need to broaden their criteria for evaluating academic research performance; not only using the number of published articles in A-listed journals but also citation counts as well as taking into account other publication outlets, such as books and book chapters. Universities, schools and departments need to revise their policies for hiring, tenure and promotion in accordance with the proposed changes in governmental evaluation practices. Journal editors and reviewers also need to reconsider a whole range of professional norms, such as 'adding-to-the-literature', conventional views of rigor and pigeonholing that drive researchers into incremental gap-spotting research. In particular, they need to develop a set of alternative norms that actively encourage less constrained work, where the value of innovative and novel ideas needs to be upgraded and the pressure to adapt to a conventional journal format and standards should occasionally be relaxed.

We, as individual researchers, must also actively cultivate a more scholarly orientation towards research. One crucial step is to engage in critical debates and reflections about what the purposes of research are and how more innovative and influential theories can be produced. A researcher identity engineered to only produce similar-looking journal articles for a limited group of sub-specialists is counterproductive to the ideal of interesting and influential studies, in which assumption-challenging is a key characteristic.

8

CONSTRUCTING INTERESTING RESEARCH QUESTIONS: PROBLEMATIZATION AND BEYOND

The aim of this chapter is to summarize the general arguments of the book. We discuss the main contributions generated by the problematization methodology and the overall framework for identifying and challenging assumptions in a research field and, based on that, constructing research questions that lead to the development of more interesting and influential theories. We also briefly address how 'non-mainstream' research questions can be generated from existing literature and supplemented by the problematization of empirical material (data), both during fieldwork and analysis. In other words, we look beyond the construction of research questions from existing studies and link up with subsequent stages of the overall research process. In addition, we discuss under what circumstances the problematization methodology can be particularly useful to apply.

Summing up the contribution of the book

Our primary aim in this book has been to encourage a more reflexive and inventive scholarship by proposing and elaborating a problematization methodology for generating research questions. In addition, we have elaborated a broader institutional and normative 'back-up' for doing more interesting, consensus-challenging, studies. We have specifically focused on how to generate more interesting research questions by problematizing the assumptions underlying existing literature in different ways. There are of course other issues involved in constructing research questions. But in order to lend sharpness to our inquiry we have refrained from trying to cover 'everything'.

In order to explore our key themes we have investigated and answered the following questions: (1) How do social researchers tend to produce their research questions in relationship to existing literature (theory and studies)? (2) Which norms are behind the dominant strategies for constructing research questions from existing literature? (3) What is seen as leading to interesting theoretical ideas? (4) How can research questions be constructed so they are more likely to lead to interesting theories? (5) Which institutions, norms and orientations are preventing researchers from doing the more interesting work and, instead, settling for incremental and often rather boring and trivial contributions? (6) How can institutions, the academic community and researchers' self-identities be changed so that they better encourage and support the development of more interesting and challenging research questions? Let us summarize and briefly add some comments on how we have answered these six questions.

(1) We have investigated how researchers construct research questions in relationship to existing literature, with an emphasis on those ways that are most likely to promote the development of interesting and influential theories. We found that gap-spotting is the dominant way of developing research questions from existing literature. It is by looking for 'gaps' – either a lack of studies or a shortage in the delivery of conclusive results in existing literature – that research questions typically are constructed. Within the overall category of gap-spotting, we identified three basic versions, namely, confusion, neglect and application-spotting. Gap-spotting seems to be the dominant approach to research problems within the areas we have investigated (education, management, psychology, sociology) and possibly within the social sciences more generally. The gap-spotting approach is symptomatic of, and related to, a broader set of problems involving specialized and narrow research practices in social science, expressed through assessments such as 'much of contemporary sociological theory has degenerated into hermeticism, sterile and self-referential discourses' (Delanty, 2005: 2).

(2) Our study suggests that while conventional research and their opponents (for example, postmodernists, critical theorists and advocates of other problematization turns) differ considerably, they often appear to converge when it comes to how they construct research questions from the existing literature. They share – or at least comply with and reproduce – a set of social norms and conventions about how to construct research questions that go beyond paradigmatic differences. We can point at a number of overlapping intellectual reasons, social norms and institutional mechanisms that strongly lead researchers to use gap-spotting for constructing research questions from existing literature: (i) gap-spotting often makes sense to use; (ii) gap-spotting is an uncontroversial and safe way of constructing research questions; (iii) the scientific ideal of knowledge accumulation means building positively on – rather than disrupting – earlier studies; (iv) research institutions strongly favor high productivity, which discourages high-risk, consensus-challenging research; (v) the contemporary journal format and forms of assessment further encourage gap-spotting; and (vi) gap-spotting is not particularly demanding while problematization as an alternative is politically as well as intellectually difficult. (We have addressed these aspects in Chapter 7, and treat them more extensively in Sandberg and Alvesson, 2011.)

In the vocabulary developed in this study, the prevalence of gap-spotting across intellectual traditions suggests that it constitutes a broadly shared assumption within many areas of social studies, perhaps even within the social sciences as a whole. It provides researchers with a shared, and to a large extent taken-for-granted, norm for generating research questions from existing theory (at least as it is presented in published texts, guiding the actual research contribution delivered). However, while gap-spotting plays a significant role in developing existing literature, it reinforces rather than challenges the assumptions underlying established theories and, thus, actually reduces the chances of producing really interesting theories. Our identification and articulation of gap-spotting as a field assumption within social research can therefore be seen as an important contribution in itself. It offers a strong signal to the research community that the grip of gap-spotting as *the* main way of constructing research questions needs to be loosened. At the same time, it encourages researchers to go beyond the logic of gap-spotting and to work with alternative ways of generating research questions that may lead to the development of more interesting theories and research results.

Without denying the relevance and advantages of gap-spotting, we believe it is important to loosen up the set of social norms that encourage researchers to use and internalize gap-spotting as the preferred way of constructing research questions from existing theory. In particular, given that challenging the assumptions that underlie existing literature (including in the researcher's own tradition) is recognized as a key aspect of what makes a theory interesting and influential, it would be in our interest to broaden our norms and methodological guidelines for knowledge production so they not only encourage gap-spotting, but also go beyond this.

(3) We have also addressed the issue of what ways of constructing research questions may lead to interesting and influential ideas and theories. Arguably, gap-spotting questions are not likely to lead to the development of interesting theories because of their failure to challenge the assumptions which underlie existing theories. Acceptance and reproduction of 'truths' means that only marginal knowledge contributions are likely to occur. We point to, and elaborate, problematization as an obvious alternative. The idea is to enable and actively promote the development of approaches that focus carefully and critically on assumptions, worldviews, perspectives, conventions, selective language and other elements with the aim of disrupting and considering alternatives to established thinking in formulating research questions. This leads to the reformulation of some basic elements of 'received wisdom' and the carving out of new, perhaps surprising and 'logic-breaking' questions.

Problematization can, and usually does, draw upon various intellectual resources, such as one or several of the 'problematization-friendly' traditions (that is, the interpretive, linguistic or social constructionist). However, a key criterion for problematization as we define the enterprise in this book – is to go beyond the application of a particular approach. Asking standard, off-the-shelf feminist questions about gender inequality, using Foucault to link knowledge and power or drawing upon process philosophy to find fluency where others construct stability are not sufficient to do problematization as we define it. This creates fairly high demands on the research and calls for some degree of originality. We are, however, still not talking about paradigm revolutions or something similarly grandiose. There are plenty of options in between piecemeal puzzle solving and suggesting an entirely new intellectual worldview.

Both gap-spotting and problematization can vary in scope and complexity. There are in most projects some elements – steps, considerations and combinations – of (minor) problematization and (some) gap-spotting. Different parts or stages in a research process may include strong elements of gap-spotting or problematization and modes of relating to the literature in relationship to the generation of a research question. Nevertheless, the major elements in gap-spotting and problematization are, as elaborated in this book, very different. They refer to distinctly different research logics. Gap-spotting expresses faith in existing studies, and the assumptions on which they are based, and strives to build positively on them. Problematization is more skeptical. It asks what may be fundamentally 'wrong' with the assumptions underlying existing studies, even those underlying one's own favorite theories, and tries to challenge them. As we have seen, very little of the latter is apparent in the crucial and final step of formulating research in research texts, that is, the communicated knowledge contribution. The extent to which problematization is used more in fieldwork or in other stages of the research process is an interesting topic, but goes beyond the scope of this book. Our guess is that problematization here is also often quite limited. One would expect that challenging dominant assumptions during the empirical work would lead to more than incremental research questions. However, the strong domination of incremental research suggests that there is not much ambitious assumption-challenging of theory during empirical work.

(4) The main contribution of this study is the proposed problematization methodology, which provides a comprehensive and systematic addition to gap-spotting and programmatic problematization. Instead of providing different strategies for identifying or constructing gaps in existing literature (and then filling them) or a prepackaged, programmatic problematization to challenge the assumptions of others, this methodology enables us to identify, articulate and challenge the different types of assumptions underlying existing literature and, based on that, to formulate research questions that may facilitate the development of more interesting and influential theories.

The methodology advocates a dialectical interrogation of our own familiar position, other theoretical stances and the literature domain targeted. It facilitates assumption-challenging in two ways. First, it offers specific heuristic support for identifying and challenging assumptions in the existing literature through its typology, consisting of five broad types of assumptions: in-house, root metaphor, paradigm, ideology and field assumptions. Second, it provides a set of specific principles for how assumptions in existing theory can be problematized and, based on that, can generate novel research questions: (i) identifying a domain of literature for assumption-challenging investigations; (ii) identifying and articulating the assumptions (in-house, root metaphor, paradigm, ideology and field assumptions) underpinning existing theory as clearly as possible; (iii) assessing them, pointing at shortcomings, problems, and oversights; (iv) developing new assumptions and formulating research questions; (v) relating the alternative assumption ground to an identified audience and assessing the audience's potential resistance and responsiveness to it; and (vi) evaluating whether the alternative assumptions are likely to generate a theory that will be seen as interesting and crafting the alternative line of inquiry in a dialogic form to increase the likelihood that readers will respond positively to it.

It is important to emphasize that the proposed methodology in itself does not guarantee a successful problematization outcome. A whole range of other factors, such as creativity, imagination, reflexivity, range of knowledge mastered and a broad understanding of different meta-theoretical standpoints, is also critical. Also rich experiences with relevant empirical material can be useful. In areas where a lot of thinking from different perspectives has been conducted it may be very difficult to come up with a novel problematization. However, taken together, the methodology presented here offers a systematic approach for generating more novel research questions through problematization of the existing literature that can be very useful and add significantly to other elements in the creative research process.

It is important to emphasize that the aim of the problematization methodology typically involves some self-questioning. The *dialectical interrogation* mentioned means that one becomes prepared to revise one's own received ideas. This is vital in order to have a good chance of identifying, articulating and challenging the different types of assumptions underlying existing literature and, based on that, to formulate research questions that may facilitate the development of more interesting and influential theories. As mentioned, formulating novel research questions through problematization involves not just using a particular preferred meta-theoretical standpoint in order to challenge the assumptions of others (as is often the case in the paradigm debates or as in various applications of critical perspectives). This ready-made or programmatic problematization can be seen as a form of 'pseudo-problematization' and only reproduces the assumptions of the framework inspiring the researcher. It is therefore unlikely to lead to particularly novel and interesting ideas, unless perhaps if one is the first to import a framework or theorist into a field unfamiliar with the source of new ideas. 'Genuine' problematization also involves questioning the assumptions underlying one's own meta-theoretical position. The ambition is, of course, not necessarily to totally un-do one's own position, only to unpack it sufficiently so that some of one's ordinary held assumptions can be scrutinized and possibly be reconsidered in the process of constructing novel research questions.

An important inspiration for this book, as well as for other authors interested in promoting interesting research, has been Davis's (1971) seminal insight that challenging assumptions is what makes a theory interesting, elaborated in his 'index of the interesting'. Our problematization methodology extends and goes beyond Davis's index in two significant ways: (i) compared to Davis's general definition of assumption ('what seems to be X is in reality non-X'), the typology of assumptions elaborated within the problematization methodology provides a more nuanced and enriched specification of which types of assumptions are available for problematization, and (ii) in contrast to Davis, the methodology offers a set of specific principles for how to identify, articulate, and challenge the assumptions underlying existing literature and, based on that, to construct interesting and novel research questions.

(5) Our study clearly shows that problematization as a key element in the construction of research questions is rarely used. This is surprising given the growing recognition that challenging assumptions is what makes a theory interesting and significant. What is more surprising, though, is that even advocates of the various 'problematization turns' (for example, interpretive, political, linguistic, constructionist and postmodernist), which actively encourage researchers to challenge assumptions and rethink received wisdom, seem to apply gap-spotting as their preferred way of constructing research questions. There are of course exceptions, and many studies include minor elements of 'problematizations', although they do not typically challenge assumptions in any ambitious sense. Gap-spotting is thus not restricted to neo-positivistic researchers. (Of course, there is plenty of critique and debate in the fields, but this is typically about advocates of one standpoint arguing against another framework in an often predictable way, not problematizing the literature one has an originally positive or 'neutral' attitude to.)

There is a widely felt disappointment with the lack of interesting and influential work in many fields. Several leading journal editors and prominent scholars have made repeated calls and attempts to change the situation but without success. They call for imaginative and challenging papers but researchers more or less voluntarily publish incremental and boring work. It is important both to understand why there is such a serious shortage of interesting and influential work in at least some fields, including our own (organization studies), despite the dramatic increase in research during the last decades, and to suggest ways forward for how more innovative and influential studies can be produced. We have addressed some elements supporting gap-spotting in this book.

We have also taken a broader perspective on the functioning of contemporary academia and identified three interplaying key drivers behind the unfortunate gap-spotting/problematization ratio and the over-focus on incremental and not so interesting studies, namely, how specific institutional policies, professional norms and researchers identity construction interplay in a way that strongly encourages and in some cases almost forces, researchers into gap-spotting research. A very strong emphasis on journal publication in highly ranked journals, the counting of the number of articles published, strong encouragement of sub-specialization and a standardized format in journals, and researchers defining themselves very much as experts in sub-fields and as (potentially) successful by publishing in the best or better journals all contribute to cautious, conventional, incremental work. The researcher comes out as an incremental gap-spotter rather than a problematizing and inventive scholar.

(6) We have proposed and discussed how specific changes in those key drivers can facilitate the development of more innovative and influential theories in social science. While the 'evil' system of institutional policies for academic ranking, professional norms and researchers' identity construction appears to be near impossible to break away from, we proposed that researchers may not be as much victims of the system as it first appears. This is because it is we ourselves, as academics, who to a large extent are the developers and executers of the 'evil' system that 'forces' us into incremental gap-spotting research, leading to the severe shortage of interesting and

influential theories in organization studies and other disciplines. We have suggested several ways by which governments, universities, schools and department as well as journal editors and reviewers can move away from a one-sided cultivation of the gap-spotting mode by more actively cultivating a more reflexive and inventive scholarship mode where consensus-challenging rather than consensus-seeking studies are emphasized. We also suggested ways for how we as individual researchers can actively cultivate a more scholarly orientation towards research, to be less cautious and instrumental, more inclined to risk-taking and a more long-term perspective. Furthermore, in order to cultivate a more scholarly attitude we urge social researchers to use and develop alternative frameworks and methodologies for developing theories with a focus on breaking away from the reproduction of established frameworks. We have in this book proposed a methodology that is specifically designed to identify and challenge the assumptions underlying existing literature and, based on that, develop more innovative and influential research. This is of course not intended to try to monopolize ways of doing interesting research, as it obviously can be done in many different ways. Here we only propose one possible methodological aid and support for moving away from some of the contemporary problems in at least some significant parts of social science.

When and why should there be problematization in generating research questions?

Given its potential to generate more interesting theories, it may be tempting to advocate a problematization methodology (as proposed in this book or the general ideal 'operationalized' in another form) as *the key* ingredient in formulating research questions.[1] There are, however, often good reasons to also consider various forms of gap-spotting routes as leading to good, although not so novel research questions, such as supplementing and enriching other studies and clarifying issues where there are diverse opinions and incoherent results. Sometimes empirical findings will play a major role in the formulation of the purpose of a study, such as in cases when one (re)formulates the research task quite late in the process (Alvesson and Kärreman, 2011). Combinations of various elements/tactics for selectively building upon and partially problematizing established literature by challenging its underlying assumptions

---

[1]To repeat, we emphasize here the formulation of research question in relationship to existing literature (theory and studies) within a domain. This is of course not the only ingredient in how a research project is framed. The good research question is important, even crucial in any project with the ambition to develop something theoretically interesting. (Strict inductive approaches like grounded theory may disagree: see Alvesson and Sköldberg, 2009 for an argumentation against the possibility to 'discover' or develop theory on purely empirical grounds.) There are, of course, other inputs to research questions and in descriptive projects with limited or no theoretical ambitions relating to the literature this is less important. But this falls outside the focus of this book.

are probably often more productive than 'purist' approaches, here meaning separating the problematization of the literature from other modes of breaking away from conventional thinking and coming up with creative ideas.

We may also remind ourselves of the risk of perpetual problematization – over-problematization – leading to a sense of fatigue and a deficit in positive results, as in the case of postmodernism (for example, deconstruction) and partly critical theory. There is a problem if more energy goes into challenging assumptions than into working out and refining or testing well-founded and productive ideas. As Barley (2006) aptly reminds us, what if the majority of researchers became committed to, and successful in, writing interesting papers?

> If being interesting requires a paper to be different, before long the field would be a mess. Every paper would take on a new topic, devise a new method, or offer a new way of seeing things. With all of us so busily striving for the next interesting paper, no subjects would be studied more than once, no methods would be refined, and no ideas would be worked through. The development of knowledge, at least in any scientific sense, would all but cease. Worse yet, because there would be no status quo to provide a measure of which new papers were interesting, the field would implode into the humdrum. At that point only by taking the risk of sticking doggedly to a topic, method, or theory could scholars rescue us from the quicksand of being interesting. In the end maybe we are quite lucky that interesting papers only come along every so often and that no one can tell us how to write more interestingly. If the world were made of candy, there could never be a Willy Wonka (Barley, 2006: 19–20)!

Having said this, given the strong mainstream tradition of identifying or constructing gaps in the existing literature with the aim of filling them, we think there is considerable room for an increased use of problematization as a methodology for constructing novel research questions that can lead to the development of more interesting and influential theories within social science. The 'risk' of academia suddenly being flooded by really interesting research publications seems small.

The proposed methodology seems particularly relevant in situations of political domination and cognitive closure that easily follow on from a dominant and established tradition. The *political* situation refers to cases where a social interest bias and/or political factors govern knowledge production rather than good ideas. But also the domination of a particular school of thought can stifle new ideas and call for politically motivated problematizations. The situation of *cognitive* closure is especially salient in research areas where a particular worldview has colonized the researchers. In such situations there is often limited critical debate and there are few counter ideas because deviant voices are silenced and people receive little support from public debates and curiosity in trying to come up with alternative views. It seems particularly important to avoid a gap-spotting, extend-the-literature logic here. The benefits of rejuvenating the field may be high, although the task is not an easy one. With a strong degree of political domination and/or cognitive closure, one needs to work hard to gain acceptance for an ambitious problematization enterprise.

Beyond the problematization of the literature– interplay with empirical work

Given our focus on problematization in relationship to the research literature – theory and studies – it is beyond the scope of this book to address the huge topic of empirical work. However, we round off this volume by briefly commenting upon the possible interplay between a problematization of the literature and doing empirical work involving a strong element of problematization of empirical material. One conventional and established way to challenge dominating theoretical ideas is the use of empirical material by seeing it as a final arbitrator of ideas and hypothesis. Falsification can thus be viewed as a source of problematization – similar to what Kuhn (1970) referred to as anomalies possibly creating problems for an established paradigm and triggering developments towards revolution. But our view of interesting research goes beyond a positivistic understanding of data as verifying or falsifying an hypothesis and data offering a straightforward input for problematization.

Constructing and solving mysteries in empirical work

Unlike many others with a strong faith in the robustness of data (like quantitative or grounded theory methodologists, celebrating discipline and diligence rather than imagination), we claim that data, or our preferred term empirical material, are simply not capable of un-ambiguously showing the right route to theory or straightforwardly screening out good ideas from bad. As we see it, the interplay between theory and empirical material is more about seeing the latter as a source of inspiration and as a partner for critical dialogue, than as a guide and ultimate arbitrator. Acknowledging the constructed nature of empirical material – which is broadly accepted in the philosophy of science (Alvesson and Sköldberg, 2009; Denzin and Lincoln, 2000; Gergen, 1978; Kuhn, 1970) – has major consequences for how we consider the theory–empirical material relationship and calls for giving up the old idea of data and theory being separate.

One key aspect here is that assumptions tend to guide all understandings of data – through theories and vocabularies producing specific worldviews that tend to order reality in a predictable way and confirm one's preconceptions. Any empirical material is sensitive to the assumptions guiding the research process producing the material. It then becomes very difficult for empirical material to kick back at assumptions, unless these are clarified, opened up and problematized, and a set of different assumptions and perspectives is invoked in the work with the production and interpretation of 'data'. Through using the problematization of established assumptions it is possible for researchers to approach field studies and other forms of empirical work in a much more open-minded manner and consider more fully the variety of ways in which we can see empirical material. This is very different from aiming to fix data through measurements or codification freezing a specific meaning and direction of a representation of some phenomenon of interest. (For a detailed exposure of how this is typically problematic, see for example, Alvesson, 2011;

Alvesson and Skoldberg, 2009; Potter and Wetherell, 1987). Such measurement or codification tends to reproduce and reinforce assumptions, although there is always some scope for the empirical material being at odds with some parts of the framework and its assumptions guiding the entire enterprise.

Crucial here is the ability to be able to challenge the value of an established theory or a framework not only when it is obviously at odds with empirical material, and to explore its weaknesses and problems in relation to the phenomena it is supposed to explicate. It means to generally open up, and to point out the need and possible directions for rethinking and developing it. In order to develop new and interesting ideas challenging dominant assumptions, it is important to mobilize empirical material in such a way that it can encourage rethinking. The idea here is not to approach the area of study as 'a site where academics can demonstrate their stance towards the world, rather than a place where the world stands as a potential empirical critique of our assumptions about it' (Miller, 2001: 226).

We consequently suggest a methodology for theory development through encounters between theoretical assumptions and empirical impressions that involve an active search for opportunities to let empirical material inspire rethinking conventional ideas and categories (developed in Alvesson and Kärreman, 2011). It is the unanticipated and the unexpected – the things that puzzle the researcher due to the deviation from what is expected – that are of particular interest in the encounter. Accordingly, theory development is stimulated and facilitated through the selective interest of what does *not* work in an existing theory, in the sense of encouraging interpretations that allow a productive and non-commonsensical understanding of ambiguous social reality in ways that differ from established frameworks and routine findings. The ideal research process then includes two key elements: (1) to create a mystery; and (2) to solve it (Asplund, 1970). A mystery is then empirical findings that deviate from what is expected and lead the researcher into a (temporary) stage of bewilderment and loss: a mystery appears when we cannot understand something, calling for a new set of ideas, deviating from established assumptions and wisdoms, in order to resolve the mystery.

The empirical material, carefully constructed, thus forms a strong impetus to rethink conventional wisdom and to find input for a possible rethinking of something, becoming less self-evident and instead surprising and calling for new ideas. However, the ideal is *not*, as in neo-positivist work, such as grounded theory (Glaser and Strauss, 1967; Strauss and Corbin, 1994), to aim for an 'intimate interaction with actual evidence' that 'produces theory which closely mirrors reality' (Eisenhardt, 1989: 547).[2] This is an effective impediment to imagination as reality-mirroring

---

[2]Neo-positivism (or post-positivism) assumes the existence of a reality that can be accurately apprehended, the observer and the observed separated, and data and theory treated as separable, although data's theory-ladenness is acknowledged. The aim is to produce generalizable results (Lincoln and Guba, 2000). Most contemporary quantitative social research and qualitative research like grounded theory (although there are different versions of the latter; see Charmaz, 2000) appears to be based on neo-positivist assumptions.

easily leads to low-abstract and trivial results. Chiefly, our goal is to explore how empirical material can be used to develop theory that is interesting, rather than obvious, irrelevant or absurd (Davis, 1971). But this calls for a more active construction of empirical material in ways that are imaginative, and not just waiting passively for data to show us the route to something interesting, as is typically the case in more conventional research. For example, careful work with data as in grounded theory is hardly sufficient to trigger the imagination and lead to really novel and challenging ideas (Alvesson and Sköldberg, 2009). Of course, all this calls for some relaxation of the pressure for conventional rigor. For an extensive description and exemplification of this methodology, see Alvesson and Kärreman (2011).

Combining problematization and mystery construction

This 'mystery methodology' for how to work with empirical material adds nicely to the problematization methodology suggested in this book. The latter opens up and adds insights on alternative assumptions that can guide research; the former can be more sensitive and imaginative as a consequence of a decreased tendency to press empirical impressions into pre-established categories and theories. The mystery methodology can also more directly encourage and fine tune assumption challenging during empirical work. In many cases, one can imagine that there are problematization elements in both the review of the literature and the construction of empirical material and that both 'parts' of the research process interact and support each other.

Research in line with the spirit of this book is typically characterized by iterations and intersections between assumption challenging in relationship to the literature and to empirical material. Ideally, a preliminary problematization of the literature leads to a specific curiosity in fieldwork, which feeds back into how the research literature is being read (and re-read), which again then informs how to address and use empirical material. It is important here to consider empirical impressions as also being a vital input and corrective to revisions of assumption challenging. New assumptions may be convincing based on a critical scrutiny of the literature, but may appear less appealing given empirical impressions. While there is hardly a one-to-one relation between assumptions and data, sometimes the latter may offer fuel for rethinking assumptions and thus productively feed into an ongoing problematization process. This process is, as we have emphasized, not just restricted to an early stage in research, leading to fixed research questions following on from a literature review, but is typically ongoing, emergent and/or shifting up to the point where the final research report or article is being delivered for publication.

Let us emphasize that not only the problematization methodology but also its fieldwork (mystery) cousin imply a somewhat different researcher identity from the common one. Both methodologies call for drawing upon a broader set of theories and vocabularies as resources for challenging dominant assumptions and constructions of empirical material, more emphasis on (self)critical and hermeneutic interpretations of the frameworks and ideas in operation and some boldness in counteracting consensus. This typically means less detailed knowledge of all that has been done within a narrowly defined field, a reluctance to divide theory and data into separate categories and address these as distinct parts and sections in a report, and facing some antagonism from defenders of an established position. In short, it calls for a shift of emphasis in researcher identity: from cultivating an incremental gap-spotting research identity to becoming a reflexive and inventive scholar, with some preferences for irony and promiscuity over a fixed, programmatic position. It also calls for some back-up of professional norms, celebrating other ideals than find and fill the gap.

Concluding remarks

Given the centrality of scrutinizing and challenging the assumptions for producing interesting and influential research, we think it is necessary to question the wide use of gap-spotting within social studies. Consensus-challenging work is important and key here is the problematization of taken-for-granted assumptions within a specific field. We certainly do not claim that this is suitable for all researchers and research, and we are not saying that problematization should generally replace gap-spotting. However, given the dominance of gap-spotting – and a general feeling that many research fields now are stronger in providing rigor than producing interesting new ideas – we would urge authors, reviewers, editors and research institutions to be less inclined to one-sidedly employ and encourage gap-spotting in formulating research questions. Instead, less reproductive and more *disruptive* modes should be promoted and used, as they are likely to lead to the development of more interesting and significant theories and research results, in other words less predictable and less boring research.

More generally, the problematization methodology also contributes to more reflective and inventive scholarship in the sense that it counteracts or supplements the domination of cautious, strongly specialized, incremental research ideals. We see this overall view on academic scholarship as our key concern and view our focus in this book as a set of provocative ideas and triggers to support this overall understanding of academic work. This is very much a plea for creativity, curiosity, boldness and intellectual commitment. As a methodology, our problematization framework encourages us to produce more novel research questions and theories by actively questioning and critically scrutinizing established knowledge in academia and in society at large. It does so by offering a distinct alternative to the dominant mode of using the literature in a field for formulating research questions. Given the current shortage of interesting and influential theories in many areas of social science, the proposed problematization methodology seems much needed. But our book as a whole, and the problematization methodology more specifically, can also be seen as an identity support. By encouraging researchers to scrutinize, interpret, critically investigate and occasionally to reconsider their own and their research fields' assumptions a more reflexive and inventive scholarly identity is being encouraged. We see a distinct need for this kind of scholarly identity in the contemporary academic climate.

A reflexive note

We realize that we may be read as two 'besserwissers' describing, analyzing and suggesting solutions from above. We may also be read as two senior academics, far removed from the situation of younger researchers striving for tenure or to establish themselves, telling others what to do, and even who to be (a scholar, not an over compliant, high-ranking journal writer wannabe). And in a sense, our text can be seen as an effort to do identity regulation (Alvesson and Willmott, 2002). Gap-spotting is inferior to problematization, a real or good academic is a scholar, intrinsically oriented towards work, focusing on novel ideas, willing to take risks and seeing research as an intellectual adventure. She or he is not a career-hungry, prestige-seeking writer for journals, willing to comply with whatever it takes in order to get the status and identity-confirmation of having published here and there.

As we are both from Sweden (a small country with less rankings and status differentiation and less publication-monitoring regimes), although one of us has lived in Australia for the last 12 years, we are less well socialized into the one-sided, journal-focused research style and are not impressed by people legitimating their work by the claim that 'only journal articles count'.[3] We are however affected by the seductive and coercive nature of journal rankings, worried about making it, feeling alienated by the gap-spotting mode and its pigeonhole mentality of doing research/managing one's career, troubled by rejections of submissions, feeling the ambivalence between integrity, reasonable responsiveness to feedback and demands and the urge to get published in A-listed journals. The line between avoiding narcissistic self-indulgence and the overestimation of one's own great ideas and contributions and prostituting oneself by doing a lot of things that are against one's values and feeling for what is good scholarship is difficult to master.

We have, however, mainly wanted to write this book to convey the feeling that something odd and problematic is going on in our field, as well as in significant parts of the social sciences as a whole. What the hell do the people in this area think they are up to? 'They' are of course 'us', but given that we have been socialized into a fairly loose and free academic culture, have done extensive work outside the mainstream gap-spotting studies and have written books as well as journal articles, this means that a confessional style of writing (Starbuck, 2006; Van Maanen, 1988) struck us as being poorly suited in this case.

---

[3] Australia offers a quite different and much more regulatory regime than Sweden.

Appendix 1

Table A.1 Basic modes of gap-spotting and their specific versions

Basic gap-spotting modes	Specific versions of basic gap-spotting modes	Reviewed journal articles
Confusion spotting	Competing explanations	Anderson and Reeb (2004; ASQ 49/2: 209–37) Burnes (2004; JMS 41/6: 977–1002) Gibbons (2004; ASQ 49/2: 238–62) Queen (2005; ASQ 50/4: 610–41) Schneper and Gullien (2004; ASQ 49/2: 263–95) Thomson and Walsham (2004; JMS 41/5: 726–47). Liu et al. (2010; AJS 115/5: 1387–434) Deuchar and Holligan (2010; SOC 44/1: 13–30) Le et al. ((2011; JAP 96/1: 113–33) Larrick et al. (2011; PS 22/4: 423–8) Ono and Watanabe (2011; PS 22/4: 472–77) Hawley–Dolan and Winners (2011; PS 22/4: 435–41) Papay (2011; AERJ 48/1: 163–93) Ready et al (2011; AERJ 48/2: 335–60) Konstantolopus et al (2011; AERJ 48/2: 361–86) Moulder et al. (2011; LI 21: 614–24) Merkt et al (2011; LI 21/6: 687–704) Paakkari et al (2011; LI 2011; 21/6: 705–14) Blatchford et al (2011; LI 21/6: 715–30)
Neglect spotting	Overlooked area	Arend (2004; JMS 41/6: 1003–27) Brown (2004; OS 25/1: 95–112) Chreim (2005; JMS 42/3: 595–23) Davenport and Leitch (2005; OS 26/11: 1603–23) Ezzamel (2004; ORG 11/4: 497–537) Hannan et al. (2003; ASQ 48/3: 399–432) Jensen (2003; ASQ 48/3: 466–97) Korczynski (2005; JMS 41/4: 575–99) Marchington and Vincent (2004; JMS 41/6: 1029–56) Meriläinen et al. (2004; ORG 11/4: 539–64) Mueller et al. (2004; OS 25/1: 75–93) Musson and Tietze (2004; JMS 41/8: 1301–23) Nicolai (2004; JMS 41/6: 951–76) Ogbonna and Wilkinson (2003; JMS 40/5: 1151–78) Sidhu et al. (2004; JMS 41/6: 914–32) Sims (2005; OS 26/11: 1625–40) Sparrowe and Liden (2005; ASQ 50/4: 505–35) Vaara et al. (2005; JMS 42/3: 572–93) Zarraga and Bonache (2005; OS 26/5: 661–81). Luke (2010; AJS 115/5: 1435–79 Hook (2010; AJS 115/5: 1480–523) Schwartz (2010; AJS 115/5: 1524–57) Spires, (2011; AJS 17/1: 1–45) Arial et al. (2011; AJS 17/1: 90–171)

Basic gap-spotting modes	Specific versions of basic gap-spotting modes	Reviewed journal articles
		Cornwell (2011; AJS 17/1: 172–208)
		Holmes (2010; SOC 44/1: 139–54)
		Burke et al. (2011; JAP 96/1: 46–70)
		Judge and Cable (2011; JAP 96/1: 95–112)
		Iddekinge et al. (2011; JAP 96/1: 13–33)
		Song et al. (2011; JAP 96/1: 151–68)
		Wiltermuth and Neale (2011; JAP 96/1: 192–201)
		Morrison et al. (2011; JAP 96/1: 193–201)
		Wann et al. (2011; PS 22/4: 429–34)
		Radford et al. (2011; LI 21: 625–35)
		Kopp and Mandl (2011; LI 21: 636–449)
		Park (2011; AERJ 48/2: 387–420)
	Under-researched	Balogun and Johnson (2005; OS 26/11: 1573–01)
		Baum et al. (2005; ASQ 50/4: 536–75)
		Brickson (2005; ASQ 50/4: 576–609)
		Case and Phillipson (2004; ORG 11/4: 473–95)
		Chan (2005; JMS 42/3: 625–72)
		Corley and Goia (2004; ASQ 49/2: 173–208)
		Javidan and Carl (2004; JMS 41/4: 665–91)
		Munir and Phillips (2005; OS 26/11: 1665–87)
		Symon (2005; OS 26/11: 1641–63)
		Tsui-Auch (2004; JMS 41/4: 693–723)
		Westphal and Khanna (2003; ASQ 48/3: 361–98)
		van Breugel et al. (2005; JMS 42/3: 539–66)
		Nahrgang et al. (2011; JAP 96/1: 71–94)
		Harrison et al. (2011; JAP 96/1: 211–20)
		Hammer et al. (2011; JAP 96/1: 134–50)
		Landers et al. (2011; JAP 96/1: 202–10)
		Chao and Liden (2011; JAP 96/1: 221–9)
		Richards and Schat (2011; JAP 96/1: 169–82)
		Stanton et al. (2011; PS 22/4: 447–53)
		Bolivar and Chrispeels (2011; AERJ 48/1: 4–38)
		O'Connor et al. (2011; AERJ 48/1: 120–62)
		Boyd et al (2011; AERJ 48/2: 303–33)
		Lowe and Boucheix (2011; LI 21: 650–63)
		Frederiksen et al. (2011; LI 21: 601–13)
		Magi et al. (2011; LI 21: 664–75)
		Vamvakoussi et al. (2011; LI 21: 676–85)
		Jitendra et al. (2011; LI 21/6: 731–45)
		Wecker, et al. (2011; LI 21/6: 746–56)
		Hedenus (2011; SOC 45/1: 22–37)
		Fox (2011; SOC 45/1: 70–85)
	Lack of empirical support	Dyck et al. (2005; JMS 42/2: 387–16)
		Tyrrell and Parker (2005; JMS 42/3: 507–37)
		Kim and White (2010; AJS 115/5: 1558–96)
		Jones et al. (2010; SOC 44/1: 103–20)
		Richler et al. (2011; PS 22/4: 464–71)
		Jadallah et al. (2011; AERJ 48/1: 194–230)
		Daly and Finnigan (2011; AERJ 48/1: 39–79)
	Lacking a specific aspect	Boyle and Williams (2011; JAP 96/1: 1–12)
		Johnson and Zaval (2011; PS 22/4: 454–9)
		Lewandowky (2011; PS 22/4: 460–3)
		DeScioli et al. (2011; PS 22/4: 442–6)

(Continued)

Table A.1 *(Continued)*

Basic gap-spotting modes	Specific versions of basic gap-spotting modes	Reviewed journal articles
Application spotting	Extending and complementing existing literature	Clegg and Courparson (2004; *JMS* 41/4: 525–47) Hancock (2005; *ORG* 12/1: 29–52) Hodgson (2005; *ORG* 12/1: 51–69) Korsczynski and Ott (2004; *JMS* 41/4: 575–99) Maguire (2004; *OS* 25/1: 113–34) Nickerson and Silverman (2003; *ASQ* 48/3: 433–65) Putnam (2004; *OS* 25/1: 35–53) Rosenthal (2004; *JMS* 41/4: 601–21) Schultze and Stabell (2004; *JMS* 41/4: 549–74) Tell (2004; *ORG* 11/4: 443–71) Watson (2004; *JMS* 41/3: 447–67) Wright and Manning (2004; *JMS* 41/4: 623–43) Zanoni and Janssens (2004; *OS* 25/1: 55–74). Oliver and O'Reilly (2010; *SOC* 44/1: 49–66) Sassatelli (2010; *SOC* 44/1: 67–83) Taylor (2010; *SOC* 44/1: 85–101) Sayer (2011; *SOC* 45/1: 7–21) Montgomery (2011; *AJS* 45/1: 46–89) Axinn et al, (2011; *AJS* 45/1: 209–58) Russell (2011; *AERJ* 48/2: 236–67)

Note: AERJ, *American Educational Research Journal*; AJS, *American Journal of Sociology*; ASQ, *Administrative Science Quarterly*; JAP, *Journal of Applied Psychology*; LI, *Learning and Instruction*; JMS, *Journal of Management Studies*; OS, *Organization Studies*; ORG, *Organization*; PS, *Psychological Science*; SOC, *Sociology*.

APPENDIX 2

Table A.2 *Summary of Davis's (1971) index of the interesting*

Characterization of a single phenomenon	*The relations between multiple phenomena*
1. Organization What seems to be a disorganized (unstructured) phenomenon is in reality an organized (structured) phenomenon OR vice versa	**8. Co-relation** What seem to be unrelated (independent) phenomena are in reality correlated (interrelated) phenomena OR vice versa
2. Composition What seem to be assorted heterogeneous phenomena are in reality composed of a single element OR vice versa	**9. Co-existence** What seem to be phenomena that can exist together are in reality phenomena which cannot exist together OR vice versa
3. Abstraction What seems to an individual phenomenon is in reality a holistic phenomenon OR vice versa	**10. Co-variation** What seems to be a positive co-variation between phenomena is in reality a negative co-variation between phenomena OR vice versa
4. Generalization What seems to be a local phenomenon is in reality a general phenomenon OR vice versa	**11. Opposition** What seem to be similar phenomena are in reality opposite phenomena OR vice versa
5. Stabilization What seems to be a stable and unchanging phenomenon is in reality an unstable and changing phenomenon OR vice versa	**12. Causation** What seems to be an independent phenomenon (variable) in a causal relation is in reality the dependent phenomenon (variable) OR vice versa
6. Function What seems to be a phenomenon that functions ineffectively as a means for the attainment of an end is in reality a phenomenon that functions effectively OR vice versa	
7. Evaluation What seems to be a bad phenomenon is in reality a good phenomenon OR vice versa	

APPENDIX 3

Abbott's main heuristic tools

Abbott's methods of discovery consist of a set of *heuristics* that can support the outlined problematization methodology in important ways. According to Abbott, heuristics provide tools 'to question what already has been said, transforming it to new ideas and views' (2004: 85).

Search heuristics are geared toward questioning and breaking out from existing thinking by bringing in and utilizing new ideas from outside a specific topic or field. Examples are to make an *analogy* by trying to understand your particular subject matter with the help of a completely different subject matter outside your field, and *borrow a method* developed and used in another field and apply it on your specific research topic.

Argument heuristics mean turning something familiar and self-evident into something unfamiliar and obscure. Examples are to *problematize the obvious* as a way to generate new and interesting research avenues, and make a *reversal*, for example, universities do not facilitate but prevent learning.

Descriptive heuristics are designed to help us imagine or perhaps better re-imagine social reality in specific ways. Examples are a *changing context*, for example, to reverse what is in the foreground to the background, and changing *levels* of analysis, for example, from a micro to a macro context.

Narrative heuristics change the way reality is portrayed. Examples are *stopping and putting in motion*, for example, something that typically is seen as static becoming something that is in motion or vice versa, and *taking and leaving contingency*, for example, arguing that a phenomenon is contingent upon something specific or by arguing that is not based on any contingency.

Fractal heuristics encompass major debates in the social sciences, such as positivism versus interpretivism, and realism versus constructionism that are 'fractals in the sense that they seem important no matter at what level of investigation we take them up' (2004: 163). These and other major debates can, according to Abbott, be used as terrific heuristic tools to produce new research ideas and problems and possibilities for research by playing them out against each other.

References

Abbott, A. (2001) *Chaos of Disciplines*. Chicago, IL: University of Chicago Press.
Abbott, A. (2004) *Methods of Discovery: Heuristics for the Social Sciences*. New York: Norton.
Adler, N.J. and Hansen, H. (2012) 'Daring to care: scholarship that supports the courage of our convictions', *Journal of Management Inquiry*, 21: 128–39.
Adler, N.J. and Harzing, A. (2009) 'When knowledge wins: transcending the sense and nonsense of academic rankings', *Academy of Management Learning & Education*, 8: 72–95.
Albert, S. and Whetten, D.A. (1985) *Organizational Identity: Research in Organizational Behavior*. Greenwich, CT: JAI Press.
Alvesson, M. (1993) *Cultural Perspectives on Organizations*. Cambridge: Cambridge University Press.
Alvesson, M. (2002) *Postmodernism and Social Research*. Buckingham: Open University Press.
Alvesson, M. (2011) 'De-essentializing the knowledge intensive firm: reflections on sceptical research going against the mainstream', *Journal of Management Studies*, 48: 1640–61.
Alvesson, M. (2013a) *The Triumph of Emptiness Consumption, higher education and work*. Oxford: Oxford University Press.
Alvesson, M. (2013b) *Understanding Organizational Culture*, 2nd edn. London: Sage.
Alvesson, M. and Billing, Y. (2009) *Understanding Gender and Organization*. London: Sage.
Alvesson, M. and Kärreman, D. (2011) *Qualitative Research and Theory Development*. London: Sage.
Alvesson, M. and Sköldberg, K. (2009) *Reflexive Methodology*, 2nd edn. London: Sage.
Alvesson, M. and Willmott, H. (2002) 'Producing the appropriate individual: identity regulation as organizational control', *Journal of Management Studies*, 39 (5): 619–44.
Alvesson, M., Ashcraft, K. and Thomas, R. (2008) 'Identity matters: reflections on the construction of identity scholarship in organization studies', *Organization*, 15: 5–28.
Alvesson, M., Hardy, C. and Harley, B. (2008) 'Reflecting on reflexivity: reappraising practice', *Journal of Management Studies*, 45: 480–501.
Anderson, R.C. and Reeb, D.M. (2004) 'Board composition: balancing family influence in S&P 500 firms', *Administrative Science Quarterly*, 49: 209–37.
Ashcraft, K.L. and Alvesson, M. (2009) 'The moving targets of dis/identification: wrestling with the reality of social construction', working paper, University of Colorado, Denver, and Lund University.
Ashforth, B. (1998) 'Becoming: how does the process of identification unfold?', in D. Whetten and C. Godfrey (eds), *Identity in Organizations*. Thousand Oaks, CA: Sage. pp. 213–22.
Ashforth, B. and Mael, F. (1989) 'Social identity theory and the organization', *Academy of Management Review*, 14: 20–39.
Asplund, J. (1970) *Om Undran Infor Samhallet*. Lund: Argos.
Astley, W.G. (1985) 'Administrative science as socially constructed truth', *Administrative Science Quarterly*, 30: 497–513.
Atkinson, C.J. and Checkland, P.B. (1984) 'Extending the metaphor "system"', *Human Relations*, 41: 709–25.
Avery, R.B. and Rendall, M.S. (2002) 'Lifetime inheritances of three generations of whites and blacks', *American Journal of Sociology*, 107: 1300–46.
Bacharach, S.B. (1989) 'Organizational theories: some criteria for evaluation', *Academy of Management Review*, 14: 496–515.
Barker, J. (1993) 'Tightening the iron cage: concertive control in self-managing teams', *Administrative Science Quarterly*, 38: 408–37.

Barley, S.R. (2006) 'When I write my masterpiece: thoughts on what makes a paper interesting', *Academy of Management Journal*, 49: 16–20.

Barnett, R. (2010) 'Being a university: future possibilities'. Public lecture at the University of Queensland, Australia.

Barrett, M. and Walsham, G. (2004) 'Making contributions from interpretive case studies: examining processes of construction and use', in B. Kaplan, D.P. Truex III, D. Wastell, et al. (eds), *Information Systems Research: Relevant Theory and Informed Practice*. Boston, MA: Kluwer Academic. pp. 293–312.

Bartunek, J.M., Rynes, S.L. and Ireland, D.R. (2006) 'What makes management research interesting, and why does it matter?', *Academy of Management Journal*, 49: 9–15.

Baruch, Y. and Holtom, B.C. (2008) 'Survey response rate levels and trends in organizational research', *Human Relations*, 61: 1139–60.

Baum, J.A. (2012) 'Bazerman, M.H. (1993) 'Fairness, social comparison, and irrationality', in J.K. Murnighan (ed.), *Social Psychology in Organizations: Advances in Theory and Research*. Englewood Cliffs, NJ: Prentice-Hall. pp. 184–203.

Bazerman, C. (1993) 'Intertextual self-fashioning: Gould and Lewontin's representation of the literature' in J. Settzer (ed.), *Understanding scientific prose*, pp. 21–40. Madison: University of Wisconsin Press.

Becker, H.S. (1998) *Tricks of the Trade: How to Think About Your Research While Doing it*. Chicago, IL: University of Chicago Press.

Bedeian, A.G. (2003) 'The manuscript review process: the proper roles of authors, referees, and editors', *Journal of Management Inquiry*, 12: 331–8.

Bedeian, A.G. (2004) 'Peer review and the social construction of knowledge in the management discipline', *Academy of Management Learning & Education*, 3: 198–216.

Bernauer, J.W. (1987) 'Michael Foucault's ecstatic thinking', in J.W. Bernauer and D. Rasmussen (eds), *The Final Foucault*. Cambridge, MA: MIT Press. pp. 45–82.

Bessant, J., Birley, S., Cooper, C., Dawnson, S., Gennard, J., Gardiner, M., Gray, A., Jones, P., Mayer, C., McGee, J., Pidd, M., Rowley, G., Saunders, J. and Stark, A. (2003) 'The state of the field in UK management research: reflections of the Research Assessment Exercise (RAE) panel', *British Journal of Management*, 14: 51–68.

Bluhm, D.J., Harman, W., Lee, T.W., et al. (2010) 'Qualitative research in management: a decade of progress', *Journal of Management Studies*. Published online.

Bouchikhi, H. and Kimberly, J.R. (2001) "It's difficult to innovate': the death of the tenured professor and the birth of the knowledge entrepreneur', *Human Relations*, 54. 77–84.

Bourdieu, P. (1979) *Outline of a Theory of Practice*. Cambridge: Cambridge University Press.

Bourdieu, P. (1996) *The Rules of Art: Genesis and Structure of the Literary Field*. Cambridge: Polity Press.

Bourdieu, P. (2004) *Science of Science and Reflexivity*. Cambridge: Polity Press.

Boyer, E. (1990) *Scholarship Reconsidered*. Princeton, NJ: Carnegie Foundation for the Advancement of Teaching.

Breslau, D. (1997) 'Contract shop epistemology: credibility and problem construction in applied social science', *Social Studies of Science*, 27: 363–94.

Brookfield, S.D. (1995) *Becoming a Critically Reflective Teacher*. San Francisco, CA: Jossey-Bass.

Brown, A. (2006) 'A narrative approach to collective identities', *Journal of Management Studies*, 43: 731–54.

Bruner, J. (1996) *The Culture of Education*. Cambridge, MA: Harvard University Press.

Brunsson, N. (2003) 'Organized hypocrisy', in B. Czarniawska and G. Sevon (eds), *The Northern Lights: Organization Theory in Scandinavia*. Copenhagen: Liber and Copenhagen Business Press. pp. 201–22.

Burawoy, M. (1979) *Manufacturing Consent*. Chicago, IL: University of Chicago Press.

Burrell, G. and Morgan, G. (1979) *Sociological Paradigms and Organisational Analysis*. Aldershot: Gower.

Butler, J. (2004) *Undoing gender*. New York: Routledge.

Callon, M. (1980) 'Struggles and negotiations of what is problematic and what is not: the socio-logics of translation', in K. Knorr, R. Krohn and R. Whitley (eds), *The Social Change*. New York: Wiley. pp. 93–125.

Camerer, C.F. and Fehr, E. (2006) 'When does "economic" man dominate social behavior?', *Science*, 6: 47–52.

Campbell, J.P., Daft, R.L. and Hulin, C. (1982) *What to Study: Generating and Developing Research Questions*. Beverly Hills, CA: Sage.

Case, P. and Phillipson, G. (2004) 'Astrology, alchemy and retro-organization theory: an astrogenealogical critique of the Myers-Briggs type indicator® ', *Organization*, 11: 473–95.

Castels, R. (1994) '"Problematization" as a mode of reading history', in J. Goldstein (ed.), *Foucault and the Writing of History*. Oxford: Blackwell. pp. 237–52.

Charmaz, K. (2000) Grounded theory: Objectivist and constructivist methods. In N.K. Denzin and Y.S. Lincoln (eds), *Handbook of Qualitative Research* (2nd edn). Thousand Oaks, CA: Sage. pp. 509–35.

Chia, R. (2000) 'Discourse analysis as organizational analysis', *Organization*, 7: 513–18.

Clark, T. and Wright, M. (2009) 'So farewell then … reflections on editing the journal of management studies', *Journal of Management Studies*, 46: 1–9.

Cliff, J., Langton, N. and Aldrich, H. (2005) 'Walking the talk? Gendered rhetoric vs. action in small firms', *Organization Studies*, 26 (1): 63–91.

Cole, S. and Cole, J.R. (1967) 'Scientific output and recognition: a study in the operation of the reward system in science', *American Sociological Review*, 32: 377–90.

Collinson, D. (2003) 'Identities and insecurities', *Organization*, 10: 527–47.

Colquitt, J.A. and Zapata-Phelan, C.P. (2007) 'Trends in theory building and theory testing: a five-decade study of the Academy of Management Journal', *Academy of Management Journal*, 50: 1261–1303.

Corley, K.G. and Gioia, D.A. (2004) 'Identity ambiguity and change in the wake of a corporate spin-off', *Administrative Science Quarterly*, 49: 173–208.

Corley, K.G. and Gioia, D.A. (2011) 'Building theory about theory building: what constitutes a theoretical contribution?', *Academy of Management Review*, 36: 12–32.

Creswell, J. W. (1998) *Qualitative Inquiry and Research Design: Choosing among Five Traditions.* Thousand Oaks, CA: Sage.

Daly, A.J. and Finnigan, K.S. (2011) 'The ebb and flow of social network ties between district leaders under high-stakes accountability', *American Educational Research Journal*, 48: 39–79.

Danny, M.D., Greenwood, R. and Prakash, R. (2009) 'What happened to organization theory?', *Journal of Management Inquiry*, 18: 273–79.

Das, H. and Long, B.S. (2010) 'What makes management research interesting? An exploratory study', *Journal of Managerial Issues*, XXII: 127–42.

Davis, M.S. (1971) 'That's interesting! Towards a phenomenology of sociology and a sociology of phenomenology', *Philosophy of Social Sciences*, 1: 309–44.

Davis, M.S. (1986) 'That's classic! The phenomenology and rhetoric of successful social theories', *Philosophy of Social Sciences*, 16: 285–301.

Davis, M.S. (1999) 'Aphorism and clichés: the generation and dissipation of conceptual charisma', *Annual Review of Sociology*, 25: 245–69.

de Rond, M. and Miller, A.N. (2005) 'Publish or perish: bane or boon of academic life?', *Journal of Management Inquiry*, 14: 321–29.

Deacon, R. (2000) 'Theory as practice: Foucault's concept of problematization', *Telos*, 118: 127–39.

Deetz, S. (1992) *Democracy in an Age of Corporate Colonization: Developments in Communication and the Politics of Everyday Life.* Albany, NY: State University of New York Press.

Deetz, S. (1996) 'Describing differences in approaches to organizational science: rethinking Burrell and Morgan and their legacy', *Organization Science*, 7: 191–207.

Delanty, G. (2005) *Social Science.* Buckingham: Open University Press.
Denzin, N.K. and Lincoln, Y.S. (eds) (2000) *Handbook of Qualitative Research*, 2nd edn. Thousand Oaks, CA: Sage.
Denzin, N.K. and Lincoln, Y.S. (2011) *The Sage Handbook of Qualitative Research*, 4th edn. Thousand Oaks, CA: Sage.
Derrida, J. (1978) *Edmund Husserl's Origin of Geometry: An Introduction.* New York: Harvester Press. (First published in 1967.)
Dewey, J. (1916) *Essays in Experimental Logic.* New York: Dover.
Dewey, J. (1938) *Logic: The Theory of Inquiry.* New York: Holt.
Dillon, J.T. (1984) 'The classification of research questions', *Review of Educational Research*, 53: 327–61.
DiMaggio, P. (1995) 'Comments on "What theory is not", *Administrative Science Quarterly*, 40: 391–97.
DiMaggio, P. and Powell, W. (1983) 'The iron cage revisited: institutional isomorphism and collective rationality in organizational fields', *American Sociological Review*, 48 (2): 147–160.
Donaldson, L. (1985) *In Defence of Organization Theory.* Cambridge: Cambridge University Press.
Dutton J., Dukerich, J. and Harquail, C. (1994) 'Organizational images and member identification', *Administrative Science Quarterly*, 43: 293–327.
Dyck, B., Starke, F.A., Mischke, G.A., et al. (2005) 'Learning to build a car: an empirical investigation of organizational learning', *Journal of Management Studies*, 42: 387–416.
Eagly, A.H. and Johannesen-Schmidt, M.C. (2001) 'The leadership styles of women and men', *Journal of Social Issues*, 57: 781–97.
Easterby-Smith, M., Thorpe, R. and Jackson, P.R. (2008) *Management Research.* Los Angeles, CA: Sage.
Eckberg, D.L., and Hill L. (1980) The paradigm concept and sociology: a critical review. In Gutting, G., and S. Bend (eds), *Paradigms and Revolutions: Applications and Appraisals of Thomas Kuhn's Philosophy of Science.* IN: University of Notre Dame Press.
Eisenhardt, K. (1989) 'Building theories from case study research', *Academy of Management Review*, 14: 532–50.
Elsbach, K. (1999) 'An expanded model of organizational identification', *Research in Organizational Behavior*, 21: 163–200.
Feyerabend, P. (1978) *Against Method.* London: Verso.
Flick, U. (2006) *An Introduction to Qualitative Research*, 3rd edn. London: Sage.
Flynn, T. (1994) 'Foucault's mapping of history', in G. Gutting (ed.), *The Cambridge Companion to Foucault.* Cambridge: Cambridge University Press.
Foucault, M. (1972) *The Archaeology of Knowledge.* New York: Pantheon Books.
Foucault, M. (1977) *Discipline and Punish: The Birth of the Prison.* New York: Random House.
Foucault, M. (1980) *Power/Knowledge.* New York: Pantheon Books.
Foucault, M. (1984) 'Space, knowledge and power', in P. Rainbow (ed.), *The Foucault Reader.* New York: Pantheon Books.
Foucault, M. (1985) *The Use of Pleasure: History of Sexuality*, vol. 2. New York: Vintage Books.
Fox, N.J. (2011) 'Boundary objects, social meanings and the success of new technologies', *Sociology*, 45: 70–85.
Freebody, P. (2003) *Qualitative Research in Education: Interaction and Practice.* London: Sage.
Freire, P. (1970) *Pedagogy of the Oppressed.* New York: Herder & Herder.
Gabriel, Y. (2005) 'Glass cages and glass palaces: Images of organizations in image conscious times', *Organization*, 12: 9–29.
Gabriel, Y. (2010) 'Organization studies: a space for ideas, identities and agonies', *Organization Studies*, 31: 757–75.

Gadamer, H.-G. (1994) *Truth and Method*. New York: Continuum. (First published in 1960.)
Galbraith, J.K. (1958) *The Affluent Society*. Boston, MA: Houghton Mifflin.
Garbett, T. (1988) *How to Build a Corporation's Identity and Project its Image*. Lexington, MA: D.C. Heath.
Geertz, C. (1973) *The Interpretation of Cultures*. New York: Basic Books.
Gergen, K. (1978) 'Toward generative theory', *Journal of Personality and Social Psychology*, 31: 1344–360.
Gergen, K. (1992) 'Organization theory in the postmodern era', in M. Reed and M. Hughes (eds), *Rethinking Organizations*. London: Sage. pp. 207–26.
Gibbons, D.E. (2004) 'Friendship and advice networks in the context of changing professional values', *Administrative Science Quarterly*, 49: 238–62.
Gibbons, M., Limoges, C., Nowotny, H., et al. (1994) *The New Production of Knowledge: The Dynamic of Science and Research in Contemporary Societies*. London: Sage.
Gioia, D., Schulz, M. and Corley, K. (2000) 'Organizational identity, image, and adaptive instability', *Academy of Management Review*, 25: 63–81.
Glaser, B.G. and Strauss, A.L. (1967) *The Discovery of Grounded Theory*. New York: Aldine.
Glick, W.H., Miller, C.C. and Cardinal, L.B. (2007) 'Making a life in the field of organization science', *Journal of Organizational Behavior*, 28: 817–35.
Golden-Biddle, K. and Azuma, J. (2010) Constructing contribution in 'Strategy as Practice'. In Golsorkhi, L. Rouleau, D. Seidl, E. Vaara (eds), *Cambridge Handbook of Strategy as Practice*. Cambridge: Cambridge University Press. pp. 79–90.
Golden-Biddle, K. and Locke, K. (2007) *Composing Qualitative Research*. Thousand Oaks, CA: Sage.
Gouldner, A.W. (1970) *The Coming Crisis of Western Sociology*. New York: Basic Books.
Grandy, G. and Mills, A.J. (2004) 'Strategy as simulacra? A radical reflexive look at the discipline and practice of strategy', *Journal of Management Studies*, 41: 1153–70.
Habermas, J. (1972) *Knowledge and the Human Interest*. London: Heinemann.
Hammer, L.B., Kossek, E.E., Kent Anger, W., Bodner, T. and Zimmerman, K.L. (2011) 'Clarifying work-family intervention processes: The roles of work-family conflict and family supportive supervisor behaviors. *Journal of Applied Psychology*, 96: 134–50.
Hannan, M.T. and Freeman, J.H. (1977) 'The population ecology of organizations', *American Journal of Sociology*, 83: 929–84.
Hargens, L.L. (2000) 'Using the literature: reference networks, reference contexts, and the social structure of scholarship', *American Sociological Review*, 65: 846–65.
Haslam, A. (2004) *Psychology of Organizations*, 2nd edn. London: Sage.
Haslam, A. and Reicher, S. (2006) 'Social identity and the dynamics of organizational life', in C. Bartel, S. Blader and A. Wrzesniewski (eds), *Identity and the Modern Organization*. New York: Lawrence Erlbaum Associates. pp. 135–66.
Hassard, J. and Keleman, M. (2002) 'Production and consumption in organizational knowledge: the case of the 'Paradigms debate'', *Organization*, 9: 331–55.
Hawley-Dolan, A. and Winners, E. (2011) 'Seeing the mind behind the art: people can distinguish abstract expressionist paintings from highly similar paintings by children, chimps, monkeys, and elephants', *Psychological Science*, 22: 435.
Heidegger, M. (1981) *Being and Time*. New York: SCM Press. (First published in 1927.)
Heijes, C. (2011) 'Cross-cultural perception and power dynamics across changing organizational and national contexts: Curacao and the Netherlands', *Human Relations*, 64 (5): 653–74.
Henrich, J., Boyd, R., Bowles, S., et al. (2005) '"Economic man" in cross-cultural perspective: behavioral experiments in 15 small-scale societies', *Behavioral and Brain Sciences*, 28: 1–61.
Henriques, J., et al. (1984) *Changing the Subject: Psychology, Social Regulation and Subjectivity*. New York: Methuen.
Hesse-Biber, S.N. and Leavy P. (2011) *The Practice of Qualitative Research*. Los Angeles, CA: Sage.

Hofstede, G. (1980) *Culture's Consequences: International Differences in Work-Related Values*. Beverly Hills, CA: Sage.

Hook, J.L. (2010) 'Gender inequality in the welfare state: sex segregation in housework, 1965–2003', *American Journal of Sociology*, 115: 1480–523.

Hostetler, K. (1994) 'Community and neutrality in critical thought: a nonobjectivist view on the conduct and teaching of critical thinking', in K.S. Walters (ed.), *Re-thinking Reason: New Perspectives in Critical Thinking*. Albany, NY: State University of New York Press. pp. 135–54.

Husen, T. (1988) 'Research paradigms in education', *Interchange*, 19/1: 2–13.

Husserl, E. (1970) *Logical Investigations*, vol. 2. London: Routledge. (First published in 1900–1901.)

Jadallah, M., Anderson, R.C., Nguyen-Jahiel, K., et al. (2011) 'Influence of a teacher's scaffolding moves during child-led small-group discussions', *American Educational Research Journal*, 48: 194–230.

Jenkins, R. (2000) 'Categorization: identity, social process and epistemology', *Current Sociology*, 48: 7–25.

Johanson, L.M. (2007) 'Sitting in your readers' chair: attending to your academic sensemakers', *Journal of Management Inquiry*, 16: 290–94.

Johnson, M.S. (2003) 'Designating opponents in empirical research: the rhetoric of "interestingness" in consumer research', *Marketing Theory*, 3: 477–501.

Jones, I.R., Leontowitsch, M. and Higgs, P. (2010) 'The experience of retirement in second modernity: generational habitus among retired senior managers', *Sociology*, 44: 103–20.

Judge, T.A. and Cable, D.M. (2011) 'When it comes to pay, do the thin win? The effect of weight on pay for men and women', *Journal of Applied Psychology*, 96: 95–112.

Knights, D. (1992) 'Changing spaces: the disruptive impact of a new epistemological location for the study of management', *Academy of Management Review*, 17: 514–36.

Knights, D. and Morgan, G. (1991) 'Corporate strategy, organizations, and subjectivity: a critique', *Organization Studies*, 12: 251–73.

Knights, D. and Willmott, H. (1989) 'Power and subjectivity at work', *Sociology*, 23: 535–58.

Knorr-Cetina, K. (1981) *The Manufacture of Knowledge: An Essay on the Constructivist and Contextual Nature of Science*. New York: Pergamon Press.

Koch, S. (1981) 'The nature and limits of psychological knowledge', *American Psychologist*, 36: 257–69.

Koopman, C. (2011) 'Foucault and pragmatism: Introductory notes on metaphilosophical methodology', *Foucault Studies*, 11: 3–10.

Kopp, B. and Mandl, H. (2011) 'Fostering argument justification using collaboration scripts and content schemes', *Learning and Instruction*, 21: 636–49.

Kuhn, T.S. (1970) *The Structure of Scientific Revolutions*. Chicago, IL: University of Chicago Press.

Kunda, G. (1992) *Engineering Culture: Control and Commitment in a High-Tech Corporation*. Philadelphia, PA: Temple University Press.

Lasch, C. (1978) *The Culture of Narcissism*. New York: Norton.

Latour, B. and Woolgar, S. (1979) *Laboratory Life: The Social Construction of Scientific Facts*. London: Sage.

Lawrence, P.A. (2008) 'Lost in publication: how measurement harms science', *Ethics in Science and Environmental Politics*, 8: 9–11.

Le, H., Oh, I., Robbins, S.B., et al. (2011) 'Too much of a good thing: curvilinear relationships between personality traits and job performance', *Journal of Applied Psychology*, 96: 113–133.

Lee, T., Mitchell, T. and Sablynski, C. (1999) 'Qualitative research in organizational and vocational behavior', *Journal of Vocational Behavior*, 55: 161–87.

Leung, K. (2007) 'The glory and tyranny of citation impact: an eastern Asian perspective', *Academy of Management Journal*, 50: 510–13.

Lincoln, Y. and Guba, E. (2000) The only generalization is: There is no generalization. In R. Gomm, M. Hammersley, and P. Foster (eds), *Case Study Method: Key Issues, key Texts*. London: Sage. pp. 27–43.

Liu, K.-Y., King, M. and Bearman, P.S. (2010) 'Social influence and the autism epidemic', *American Journal of Sociology*, 115: 1387–434.

Locke, K. and Golden-Biddle, K. (1997) 'Constructing opportunities for contribution: structuring intertextual coherence and "problematizing" in organizational studies', *Academy of Management Journal*, 40: 1023–62.

Luke, N. (2010) 'Migrants' competing commitments: sexual partners in urban Africa and remittances to the rural origin', *American Journal of Sociology*, 115: 1435–479.

Lüscher, L.S. and Lewis, M.W. (2008) 'Organizational change and managerial sensemaking: working through paradox', *Academy of Management Journal*, 51: 221–40.

Macdonald, S. and Kam, J. (2007) 'Aardvark et al.: quality journals and gamesmanship in management studies', *Journal of Information Science*, 33: 702–17.

Mägi, K., Lerkkanen, M., Poikkeus, A., et al. (2011) 'The cross-lagged relations between children's academic skill development, task-avoidance, and parental beliefs about success', *Learning and Instruction*, 21: 664–75.

Mahrer, A.R. (2000) 'Philosophy of science and the foundations of psychotheraphy', *American Psychologist*, 55: 1117–125.

March, J. and Olsen, J. (1976) *Ambiguity and Choice in Organizations*. Bergen: Unversitetsforlaget.

Martin, J. (2002) *Organizational Culture: Mapping the Terrain*. Thousand Oaks, CA: Sage.

Martin, J. and Meyerson, D. (1988) 'Organizational culture and the denial, channeling and acknowledgment of ambiguity', in L.R. Pondy (ed.), *Managing Ambiguity and ambiguity*. New York: Wiley. pp. 93–125.

McCall, L. (2005) 'Gender, race, and the restructuring of work: organizational and institutional perspectives', in. S. Ackroyd, R. Batt, P. Thomson, P.S. Tolbert (eds), *The Oxford Handbook of Work & Organization*. Oxford: Oxford University Press. pp. 74–92.

McKinley, W., Mone, M.A. and Moon, G. (1999) 'Determinants and development of schools in organization theory', *Academy of Management Review*, 24: 634–48.

McMullen, J. and Shepard, D. (2006) 'Encouraging consensus challenging research in universities', *Journal of Management Studies*, 43: 1643–670.

McSweeney, B. (2002) 'Hofstede's model of national cultural differences and their consequences: a triumph of faith– a failure analysis', *Human Relations*, 55: 89–118.

Merleau-Ponty, M. (1962) *Phenomenology of Perception*. London: Routledge and Kegan Paul. (First published in 1945.)

Meyer, J. and Rowan, B. (1977) 'Institutionalized organizations: formal structure as myth and ceremony', *American Journal of Sociology*, 83: 340–63.

Miller, D. (2001) 'The poverty of morality', *Journal of Consumer Culture*, 1: 225–243.

Miller, F., Greenwood, R. and Prakash, R. (2009) 'What happened to organization theory?' *Journal of Management Inquiry*, 18: 273–79.

Mills, C.W. (1959) *The Sociological Imagination*. Oxford: Oxford University Press

Mizruchi, M.S. and Fein, L.C. (1999) 'Preview the social construction of organizational knowledge: a study of the uses of coercive, mimetic, and normative isomorphism', *Administrative Science Quarterly*, 44: 653–83.

Morgan, G. (1980) 'Paradigms, metaphors, and puzzle solving in organization theory', *Administrative Science Quarterly*, 25: 605–22.

Morgan, G. (1986) *Images of Organization*. Thousand Oaks, CA: Sage.

Morrison, E.W., Wheeler-Smith, S.L. and Kamdar, D. (2011) 'Speaking up in groups: a cross-level study of group voice climate and voice', *Journal of Applied Psychology*, 96: 183–91.

Mulkay, M. and Gilbert, N.G. (1983) 'Scientists' theory talk', *Canadian Journal of Sociology*, 8: 179–97.

Musson, G. and Tietze, S. (2004) 'Places and spaces: the role of metonymy in organizational talk', *Journal of Management Studies*, 41: 1301–323.

Myers, G. (1993) 'Making enemies: how Gould and Lewontin criticize', in J. Selzer (ed.), *Understanding Scientific Prose*. Madison, WI: University of Wisconsin Press. pp. 256–75.

Newton, T. (1998) 'Theorizing subjectivity in organizations: the failure of Foucauldian studies?', *Organization Studies*, 19: 415–47.

O'Connor, E.E., Dearing, E. and Collins, B.A. (2011) 'Teacher-child relationship and behavior problem trajectories in elementary school', *American Educational Research Journal*, 48: 120–62.

Oliver, C. and O'Reilly, K. (2010) 'A Bourdieusian analysis of class and migration: habitus and the individualizing process', *Sociology*, 44: 49–66.

Palmer, D. (2006) 'Taking stock of the criteria we use to evaluate one another's work: ASQ 50 years out', *Administrative Science Quarterly*, 51: 535–59.

Papay, P.J. (2011) 'Different tests, different answers: the stability of teacher value-added estimates across outcome measures', *American Educational Research Journal*, 48: 163–93.

Penfold-Mounce, R., Beer, D. and Burrows, R. (2011) '*The Wire* as social science-fiction?', *Sociology*, 45: 152–67.

Peter, P.J. and Olson, J.C. (1986) 'Is science marketing?', *Journal of Marketing*, 47: 111–25.

Pfeffer, J. (1993) 'Barriers to the advance of organizational science: paradigm', *Academy of Management Review*, 18: 599–620.

Pfeffer, J. (2007) 'A modest proposal: how we might change the process and product of managerial research', *Academy of Management Journal*, 50: 1334–345.

Pierson, P. (2007) 'The cost of marginalization: qualitative studies of American politics', *Comparative Political Studies*, 40: 145–69.

Potter, J. and Wetherell, M. (1987) *Discourse and Social Psychology: Beyond Attitudes and Behaviour*. London: Sage.

Pratt, M. (2000) 'The good, the bad, and the ambivalent: managing identification among Amway distributors', *Administrative Science Quarterly*, 45: 456–93.

Pratt, M. (2009) 'From the editors: the lack of a boilerplate: tips on writing up (and rewriting) qualitative research', *Academy of Management Journal*, 52: 856–62.

Pratt, M. and Foreman, P. (2000) 'Classifying responses to multiple organizational identities', *Academy of Management Review*, 25: 18–42.

Richardson, F.C. and Slife, B.D. (2011) 'Critical thinking in social and psychological inquiry', *Journal of Theoretical and Philosophical Psychology*, 31 (3): 165–72.

Richler, J.J. Cheung, O. S. and Gauthier, I. (2011) 'Holistic processing predicts face recognition', *Psychological Science*, 22: 464–71.

Ritchie, J. (2003) 'The applications of qualitative methods to social research', in J. Ritchie and J. Lewis (eds), *Qualitative Research Practice*. London: Sage. pp. 24–46.

Ritzer, G. (1980) *Sociology: A Multiple Paradigm Science*. Boston, MA: Allyn and Bacon.

Ritzer, G. (1998) 'Writing to be read: changing the culture and reward structure of American sociology', *Contemporary Sociology*, 27: 446–53.

Rorty, R. (1992) 'Cosmopolitanism without emancipation: a response to Lyotard', in S. Lash and J. Friedman (eds), *Modernity & Identity*. Oxford: Blackwell. pp. 59–72.

Rosenau, P.M. (1992) *Post-Modernism and the Social Sciences: Insights, Inroads and Intrusions*. Princeton, NJ: Princeton University Press.

Russell, J.L. (2011) 'From child's garden to academic press: the role of shifting institutional logics in redefining kindergarten education', *American Educational Research Journal*, 48: 236–67.

Rynes, S.L. (2007) 'Academy of management journal editor's forum on rich research: editor's foreword', *Academy of Management Journal*, 50: 13.

Sandberg, J. (2000) 'Understanding human competence at work: an interpretive approach', *Academy of Management Journal*, 43: 9–25.

Sandberg, J. (2001) 'The constructions of social constructionism', in S. E. Sjöstrand, J. Sandberg, and M. Tyrstrup (eds), *Invisible Management: The Social Construction of Leadership*. London: Thomson. pp. 29–48.

Sandberg, J. and Alvesson, M. (2011) 'Ways of constructing research questions: gap-spotting or problematization?', *Organization*, 18: 23–44.

Sandberg, J. and Targama, A. (2007) *Managing Understanding in Organizations*. London: Sage.

Sandberg, J. and Tsoukas, H. (2011) 'Grasping the logic of practice: theorizing through practical rationality', *Academy of Management Review*, 36: 338–60.

Sauder, M. and Espeland, W.E. (2009) 'The discipline of rankings: tight coupling and organizational change', *American Sociological Review*, 74: 63–82.

Savin-Baden, M. and Major, C. (2012) *Qualitative Research: The Essential Guide to Theory and Practice*. London: Routledge.

Sayer, A. (2011) 'Habitus, work and contributive justice', *Sociology*, 45: 7–21.

Schein, E. (1985) *Organization Culture and Leadership*. San Francisco, CA: Jossey-Bass.

Schultze, U. and Stabell, C. (2004) 'Knowing what you don't know? Discourses and contradictions in knowledge management research', *Journal of Management Studies*, 41: 549–73.

Sennett, R. (1998) *The Corrosion of Character*. New York: Norton.

Shotter, J. and Gergen, K. (eds) (1989) *Texts of Identity*. London: Sage.

Sievers, B. (1986) 'Beyond the surrogate of motivation', *Organization Studies*, 7: 335–51.

Silverman, D. (2001) *Interpreting Qualitative Data*, 2nd edn. London: Sage.

Simon, H.A. (1947) *Administrative Behavior: A Study of Decision-Making Processes in Administrative Organization*. New York: Macmillan.

Singh, G., Haddad, K.M. and Chow, C.W. (2007) 'Are articles in "top" management journals necessarily of higher quality?', *Journal of Management Inquiry*, 16: 319–31.

Slife, B.D. and Williams, R.N. (1995) *What's Behind the Research? Discovering Hidden Assumptions in the Behavioral Sciences*. Thousand Oaks, CA: Sage.

Smircich, L. (1983) 'Concepts of culture and organizational analysis', *Administrative Science Quarterly*, 28: 339–58.

Stacey, J. (1999) 'Virtual truth with a vengeance', *Contemporary Sociology*, 28: 18–23.

Starbuck, W.H. (2003) 'Turning lemons into lemonade: where is the value in peer reviews?', *Journal of Management Inquiry*, 12: 344–51.

Starbuck, W.H. (2006) *The Production of Knowledge: The Challenge of Social Science Research*. Oxford: Oxford University Press.

Starbuck, W.H. (2009) 'The constant causes of never-ending faddishness in the behavioral and social sciences', *Scandinavian Journal of Management*, 25: 108–16.

Steier, F. (ed) (1991) *Research and Reflexivity: Inquiries in Social Construction*. Thousand Oaks, CA: Sage.

Stevens, M.L., Armstrong, E.A. and Arum, R. (2008) 'Sieve, incubator, temple, hub: empirical and theoretical advances in the sociology of higher education', *Annual Review of Sociology*, 34: 127–51.

Strauss, A. and Corbin, J. (1994) 'Grounded theory methodology: an overview', in N.K. Denzin and Y.S. Lincoln (eds), *Handbook of Qualitative Research*. Thousand Oaks, CA: Sage. pp. 273–85.

Sutton, R. and Staw, B. (1995) 'What theory is not', *Administrative Science Quarterly*, 40: 371–84.

Taylor, N. (2010) 'Animal shelter emotion management: a case of in situ hegemonic resistance?', *Sociology*, 44: 85–101.

Tsang, E.W.K. and Frey, B.S. (2007) 'The as-is journal review process: let authors own their ideas', *Academy of Management Learning & Education*, 6: 128–36.

Tsoukas, H. and Chia, R. (2002) 'On organizational becoming: rethinking organizational change', *Organization Science*, 13: 567–82.

Tsoukas, H. and Knudsen, C. (eds) (2004) *The Oxford Handbook of Organization Theory*. Oxford: Oxford University Press.

Vaara, E., Tienari, J., Piekkari, R., et al. (2005) 'Language and the circuits of power in a merging multinational corporation', *Journal of Management Studies*, 42: 595–623.

Van de Ven, A.H. (2007) *Engaged Scholarship: A Guide for Organizational and Social Research*. New York: Oxford University Press.

Van Maanen, J. (1988) *Tales of the Field: on Writing Ethnography*. Chicago: University of Chicago.

Van Maanen, J. and Barley, S.R. (1984) 'Occupational communities: culture and control in organizations', *Research in Organizational Behavior*, 6: 287–365.

Watson, T.J. (2004) 'HRM and critical social science analysis', *Journal of Management Studies*, 41; 447–67.

Weedon, C. (1987) *Feminist Practice and Poststructuralist Theory*. Oxford: Blackwell.

Weick, K.E. (1989) 'Theory construction as disciplined imagination', *Academy of Management Review*, 14: 516–31.

Weick, K.E. (2001) 'Gapping the relevance gap: fashions meet fundamentalist in management research', *British Journal of Management*, 12: 71–75.

Weinstein, J. (2000) 'A (further) comment on the difference between applied and academic sociology', *Contemporary Sociology*, 29: 344–47.

West, C. and Zimmerman, D.H. (1987) 'Doing gender', *Gender and Society*, 1: 125–51.

West, C. and Zimmerman, D.H. (2009) 'Accounting for doing gender', *Gender and Society*, 23: 112–22.

Westphal, J.D. and Khanna, P. (2003) 'Keeping directors in line: social distancing as a control mechanism in the corporate elite', *Administrative Science Quarterly*, 48: 361–98.

White, P. (2009) *Developing Research Questions*. New York: Palgrave.

Wicker, A.W. (1985) 'Getting out of our conceptual ruts', *American Psychologist*, 40: 1094–1103.

Wilhite, A.W. and Fong, E.A. (2012) 'Coercive citation in academic publishing', *Science*, 335: 542–43.

Willmott, H. (1993) 'Strength is ignorance; slavery is freedom: managing culture in modern organizations', *Journal of Management Studies*, 30: 515–52.

Willmott, H. (1995) 'Managing the academics: commodification and control in the development of university education in the UK', *Human Relations*, 48: 993–1027.

Willmott, H. (2011) 'Journal list fetishism and the perversion of scholarship: reactivity and the ABS list', *Organization*, 18: 429–442.

Yanchar, S.C., Slife, B.D. and Warne, R. (2008) 'Critical thinking as disciplinary practice', *Review of General Psychology*, 12: 265–81.

Yukl, G. (1999) 'An evaluation of conceptual weaknesses in transformational and charismatic leadership theories', *Leadership Quarterly*, 10: 285–305.

Yukl, G. (2006) *Leadership in Organizations*, 6th edn. Upper Saddle River, NJ: Pearson/Prentice-Hall.

Index

Page numbers in *italics* refer to tables.

Abbott, A. 2, 48, 50, 58, 59, 63, 64, 68, 128
accumulation norm 97–8
Adler, N.J. and Hansen, H. 12, 20
alternative assumptions
　development 63–5, 66–7, 75–7, 87–8
　evaluation 67–9, 78–9, 89–91
Alvesson, M. 59, 87
　and Billing, Y. 86
　et al. 7, 94
　and Kärreman, D. 16, 22, 117, 120
　and Sköldberg, K. 7, 49–50, 59, 107, 121
　and Willmott, H. 100, 123
analogies 64
Anderson, R.C. and Reeb, D.M. 29–30
application spotting 33–4, *126*
assumptions
　challenging 38–41, 44–5, 51–3
　developing alternative 63–5, 66–7, 75–7, 87–8
　identifying and articulating 58–61, 73–4, 81–3
　in relation to audience 65–7, 77–8, 89
　typology 53–6, 59–60
　see also evaluation
audience, assumptions in relation to 65–7, 77–8, 89

Bacharach, S.B. 51
Bourdieu, P. 44, 78, 94, 97

Campbell, J.P. et al. 1
challenging assumptions 38–41, 44–5, 51–3
citations/references 98
Clark, T. and Wright, M. 3
Colquitt, J.A. and Zapata-Phelan, C.P. 42, 51
combination of gap-spotting modes 34
comparative/second-order questions 15
confusion spotting 29–31, *124*
Corley, K.G. and Gioia, D.A. 4–5, 32, 41, 68
counter-induction 63–4
crediting norm 98
critical confrontation 35

Daly, A.J. and Finnigan, K.S. 34
Davis, M.S. 4, 38–41, 51, 53, 60, 67–8, 78, 89, 94, 115, 121, *127*
decision-making models 64–5
descriptive questions 14–15
Dewey, J. 51
dialectical interrogation 49–50, 114–15

Dillon, J.T. 14–15
Dutton, J. et al. 71, 72–4, 75, 76, 78–9
Dyck, B. et al. 33

empirical material 62
　and problematization methodology 119–21
　as source of research questions 18–19
evaluation
　alternative assumptions 67–9, 78–9, 89–91
　articulated assumptions 61–3, 74–5, 83–7
existing literature
　challenges to 12–13
　shortage of high-impact research 3–4
　as source of research questions 17–18, 24–7
　see also gap-spotting in existing literature; identification
explanatory/third-order questions 15

fashionable topics 19–20, 25
Feyerabend, P. 53, 57, 63
field assumptions 55, 60
Foucault, M. 37, 50, 51, 52, 88, 98, 107
Fox, N.J. 32
funding, influence of 20

Gabriel, Y. 36, 98, 100, 108
Gadamer, H.-G. 11, 13, 95
gap-spotting in existing literature
　drivers 95–100, 116–17
　explanations 101–4
　method and research design 28–9
　prevalence 41–3, 92–5
　and problematization 5–7, 36–7, 112–14, 116, 123
　recommendations for reform 104–8
　typology 29–34, *124–6*
　within and beyond 34–7
gender study 80–91
Gibbons, D.E. 30
Gioia, D.
　Corley, K.G. and 4–5, 32, 41, 68
　et al. 74, 75, 77
governments 105

Habermas, J. 20–1, 54
Hawley-Dolan, A. and Winners, E. 30–1

Heijes, C. 36
heuristic tools 128
Hofstede, G. 36

identification
    and articulating assumptions 58–61, 73–4, 81–3
    existing literature 57–8, 72–3, 80–1
identity
    organizations study 72–9
    researchers 99–100, 107–8, *109*
ideology assumptions 55, 59–60
in-house assumptions 54, 55–6, 59, 60
influential factors 19–21
influential and innovative research 104–8
institutional conditions 95–6, 105–6
interaction of sources of research questions 19
interesting theories
    characteristics (index of the interesting) 38–41, *127*
    and non-interesting theories, difference between 4–7
    and prevalence of gap-spotting 41–3, 92–5
inventive and reflexive scholarship 108, *109*

Jadallah, M. et al. 33
journals
    influence of 20, 123
    see also existing literature; gap-spotting in existing literature
Judge, T.A. and Cabel, D.M. 32

knowledge development 10–11
knowledge interest of researcher 20–1
Kopp, B. and Mandl, H. 32

Liu, K.-Y. et al. 30
Locke, K. and Golden-Biddle, K. 26–7, 28, 41, 42, 43, 57, 66–7
Luke, N. 31

mystery construction and problematization methodology 121–2

neglect spotting 31–3, *124–6*
new ideas 35–6, 62
normative questions 15
norms, professional 96–9, 106–7

O'Connor, E.E. et al. 32–3
Oliver, C. and O'Reilly, K. 34
openness 13–14

Papay, P.J. 31
paradigm camps, gap-spotting in 43
paradigmatic assumptions 54–5, 59
path-defining research 58

personal experience: as source of research questions 16–17
perspective shifting 60–1
pigeonholing 96–7
Pratt, M. 42, 74, 75, 77
problematization methodology
    aim 47–50, 114–15
    benefits and risks 117–18
    and empirical material 119–21
    and gap-spotting 5–7, 36–7, 112–14, 116, 123
    and key elements 69–70
    and mystery construction 121–2
    principles 56–69
    studies 72–9, 80–91
    see also assumptions; evaluation
professional norms 96–9, 106–7
purpose of study 15–16

quantitative and qualitative research, gap-spotting in 42

references/citations 98
reflexive and inventive scholarship 108, *109*
reform, recommendations for 104–8
research question
    criteria 11–14
    formulation process 21–2
    influential factors 19–21
    origins 16–19
    priority in knowledge development 10–11
    types 14–16
researchers
    identity construction 99–100, 107–8, *109*
    influence and interest of 20–1
reversal 64
Richler, J.J. et al. 33
rigor 96, 107
root metaphor assumptions 54, 55–6, 59
Russell, J.L. 34
Rynes, S.L. 108

Schultze, U. and Stabell, C. 34
second-order/comparative questions 15
Slife, B.D. and Williams, R.N. 49
society: as source of research questions 16
Starbuck, W.H. 44, 97, 102

Taylor, N. 34
text: issues and strategies 26–7, 43–5
theory
    definition 51
    see also interesting theories
third-order/explanatory questions 15
truth 62

university and departmental policies 105–6

victim-of-the-system explanation 101–2

Watson, T.J. 33, 43

we are in-charge-of-the-system explanation 102–4

West, C. and Zimmerman, D.H. 71, 80–3, 84, 85, 86, 88, 89, 90

White, P. 11, 15, 16, 18, 21